Angels in the Bible

Angels in the Bible

George M. Smiga

with Little Rock Scripture Study staff

Little Rock
Scripture Study

LITURGICAL PRESS
Collegeville, Minnesota

www.littlerockscripture.org

Nihil obstat: Reverend Robert C. Harren, J.C.L., *Censor deputatus*.
Imprimatur: ✠ Most Reverend Donald J. Kettler, J.C.L., Bishop of St. Cloud, Minnesota. September 1, 2020.

Cover design by John Vineyard. Interior art by Ned Bustard. Photo and illustrations on pages 34, 47, 101, and 104 courtesy of Getty Images.

 This symbol indicates material that was created by Little Rock Scripture Study to supplement the biblical text and commentary. Some of these inserts first appeared in the *Little Rock Catholic Study Bible*; others were created specifically for this book by Michael DiMassa and George M. Smiga.

5   6   7   8   9

Library of Congress Cataloging-in-Publication Data

Names: Smiga, George M., 1948- author. | Little Rock Scripture Study Staff, contributor.
Title: Angels in the Bible / George M. Smiga with Little Rock Scripture Study Staff.
Description: Collegeville, Minnesota : Liturgical Press, [2021] | Series: Little Rock scripture study | Summary: "In Angels in the Bible, George Smiga examines some of the Bible's passages about angels, exploring their ministry on God's behalf and drawing insights for our own spiritual lives. Because angels are mediators of God's presence and action, studying angels is studying God"-- Provided by publisher.
Identifiers: LCCN 2020036842 (print) | LCCN 2020036843 (ebook) | ISBN 9780814665596 (paperback) | ISBN 9780814665848 (epub) | ISBN 9780814665848 (mobi) | ISBN 9780814665848 (pdf)
Subjects: LCSH: Angels--Biblical teaching. | Angels--Christianity. | Guardian angels.
Classification: LCC BS680.A48 S65 2021 (print) | LCC BS680.A48 (ebook) | DDC 235/.3--dc23
LC record available at https://lccn.loc.gov/2020036842
LC ebook record available at https://lccn.loc.gov/2020036843

TABLE OF CONTENTS

Wrap-Up Lectures and Discussion Tips for Facilitators are available for each lesson at no charge. Find them online at LittleRockScripture.org/Lectures/AngelsintheBible.

Welcome

The Bible is at the heart of what it means to be a Christian. It is the Spirit-inspired word of God for us. It reveals to us the God who created, redeemed, and guides us still. It speaks to us personally and as a church. It forms the basis of our public liturgical life and our private prayer lives. It urges us to live worthily and justly, to love tenderly and wholeheartedly, and to be a part of building God's kingdom here on earth.

Though it was written a long time ago, in the context of a very different culture, the Bible is no relic of the past. Catholic biblical scholarship is among the best in the world, and in our time and place, we have unprecedented access to it. By making use of solid scholarship, we can discover much about the ancient culture and religious practices that shaped those who wrote the various books of the Bible. With these insights, and by praying with the words of Scripture, we allow the words and images to shape us as disciples. By sharing our journey of faithful listening to God's word with others, we have the opportunity to be stretched in our understanding and to form communities of love and learning. Ultimately, studying and praying with God's word deepens our relationship with Christ.

Angels in the Bible

The resource you hold in your hands is divided into six lessons. Each lesson involves personal prayer and study using this book *and* the experience of group prayer, discussion, and wrap-up lecture.

If you are using this resource in the context of a small group, we suggest that you meet six times, discussing one lesson per meeting. Allow about 90 minutes for the small group gathering. Small groups function best with eight to twelve people to ensure good group dynamics and to allow all to participate as they wish.

Some groups choose to have an initial gathering before their regular sessions begin. This allows an opportunity to meet one another, pass out books, and, if desired, view the optional intro lecture for this study available on the "Resources" page of the Little Rock Scripture Study website (www.littlerockscripture.org).

Every Bible study group is a little bit different. Some of our groups like to break each lesson up into two weeks of study so they are reading less each week and have more time to discuss the questions together at their weekly gatherings. If your group wishes to do this, simply agree how much of each lesson will be read each week, and only answer the questions that correspond to the material you read. Wrap-up lectures can then be viewed at the end of every other meeting rather than at the end of every meeting. Of course, this will mean that your study will last longer, and your group will meet more times.

WHAT MATERIALS WILL YOU USE?

The materials in this book include:

- Commentary by George M. Smiga.
- Occasional inserts 🔥 highlighting elements of the Scripture being studied. Some of these appear also in the Little Rock Catholic Study Bible while others are supplied by the author and staff writers.
- Questions for study, reflection, and discussion at the end of each lesson.
- Opening and closing prayers for each lesson, as well as other prayer forms available in the closing pages of the book.

In addition, there are wrap-up lectures available for each lesson. Your group may choose to purchase a DVD containing these lectures or make use of the audio or video lectures online at no charge. The link to these free lectures is: LittleRockScripture.org/Lectures/AngelsintheBible. Of course, if your group has access to qualified speakers, you may choose to have live presentations.

Each person will need a current translation of the Bible. We recommend the *Little Rock Catholic Study Bible*, which makes use of the New American Bible, Revised Edition. Other translations, such as the New Jerusalem Bible or the New Revised Standard Version: Catholic Edition, would also work well.

HOW WILL YOU USE THESE MATERIALS?

Prepare in advance

Using Lesson One as an example:

- Begin with a simple prayer like the one found on page 11.
- Read the assigned material in the printed book for Lesson One (pages 12–20) so that you are prepared for the

weekly small group session. You may do this assignment by reading a portion over a period of several days (effective and manageable) or by preparing all at once (more challenging).

- Answer the questions, Exploring Lesson One, found at the end of the assigned reading, pages 21–23.

- Use the Closing Prayer on page 24 when you complete your study. This prayer may be used again when you meet with the group.

Meet with your small group

- After introductions and greetings, allow time for prayer (about 5 minutes) as you begin the group session. You may use the prayer found on page 11 (also used by individuals in their preparation) or use a prayer of your choosing.

- Spend about 45–50 minutes discussing the responses to the questions that were prepared in advance. You may also develop your discussion further by responding to questions and interests that arise during the discussion and faith-sharing itself.

- Close the discussion and faith-sharing with prayer, about 5–10 minutes. You may use the Closing Prayer at the end of each lesson or one of your choosing at the end of the book. It is important to allow people to pray for personal and community needs and to give thanks for how God is moving in your lives.

- Listen to or view the wrap-up lecture associated with each lesson (10–15 minutes). You may watch the lecture online, use a DVD, or provide a live lecture by a qualified local speaker. This lecture provides a common focus for the group and reinforces insights from each lesson. You may view the lecture together at the end of the session or, if your group runs out of time, you may invite group members to watch the lecture on their own time after the discussion.

Above all, be aware that the Holy Spirit is moving within and among you.

Angels in the Bible

LESSON ONE

Studying Angels Is Studying God

Begin your personal study and group discussion with a simple and sincere prayer such as:

Prayer

God of heaven and earth, may our time of study and reflection lead us to imitate the angels as heralds of your word and proclaimers of your glory.

Read pages 12–20, Lesson One.

Respond to the questions on pages 21–23, Exploring Lesson One.

The Closing Prayer on page 24 is for your personal use and may be used at the end of group discussion.

STUDYING ANGELS IS STUDYING GOD

It is not easy to study angels. Angels are spiritual, immaterial, and invisible beings. They cannot be weighed or examined. They live beyond our senses. A study of angels, therefore, cannot be an investigation of angels themselves. It must rather review the way the Bible presents angels to us. That is what this book attempts to provide. We will examine Scripture passages in which angels are present and discuss not only what we can learn about angels but also what we can discover about the relationship between God and ourselves.

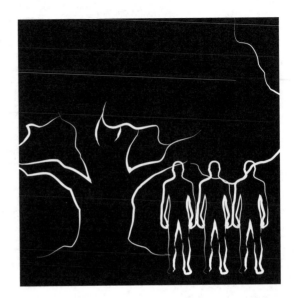

 The *Catechism of the Catholic Church* affirms that "the existence of the **spiritual, non-corporeal beings** that Sacred Scripture usually calls 'angels' is a truth of faith" supported by both Scripture and tradition. The catechism further explains that "as purely spiritual creatures, angels have intelligence and will: they are personal and immortal creatures, surpassing in perfection all visible creatures, as the splendour of their glory bears witness" (328, 330).

We are all aware of angels within our faith tradition. Some readers may even have a personal devotion to them. This study honors the belief in angels, even as it seeks to expand our appreciation of them. It is my hope that as we compare our personal understanding of angels with the portrayal of them offered in the Bible, we will allow ourselves to be stretched to view angels in new ways. In this process, the ministries that angels perform as God's agents will be more clearly identified and more deeply valued.

Like many other aspects of the Christian faith, belief in angels derives from Judaism. Angels appear throughout the Hebrew Bible (Old Testament). Their presentation, however, differs widely in description and function. This is understandable when we understand that the Jewish belief in angels developed over centuries. We will find that the earliest passages in this development present angels in ways that can be elusive and confusing. However, as the Jewish understanding of angels progressed over time, ideas about angels became more consistent and concrete. This mature understanding of angels was adopted by Jesus and the early Christian preachers who made it a part of their teaching.

What do angels look like? Most biblical passages in which angels appear provide little description of them. Very often we are simply presented with "a man," "a being," or "a messenger" who appears and then begins to act. As we will see, some passages describe angels as having bodies or physical features such as wings (thus the common representations in art and culture of angels as winged creatures). Yet it is important to remember that these are human efforts to describe angels. Such representations do not mean that angels actually have bodies or wings.

Locating biblical passages in which angels appear is complicated by terminology. There is no single Hebrew word in the Old Testament which identifies an angel. Instead there are a variety of terms that refer to beings of heavenly status who are distinct from God and humans. Often we can only detect the presence of an angel from the context or activity within a particular passage.

Sometimes angels are called "sons of God." For example, Job 38:7 says that "the morning stars sang together / and all the sons of God shouted for joy," and Psalm 29:1-2 declares, "Give to the LORD, you sons of God, / give to the LORD glory and might; / Give to the LORD the glory due his name. / Bow down before the LORD's holy splendor!"

 Since **the creation of the angels** is not mentioned explicitly in the Bible, there has been some controversy as to when this event might have occurred. In the Jewish tradition, there is almost universal agreement that angels were created sometime during the six-day account of creation found in Genesis. The apocryphal book 2 Enoch states that the angels were created on the second day when their dwelling—the "firmament"—was also created. Some rabbis, however, taught that the angels were created on the fifth day, when God made all the other winged creatures. In the Christian tradition, though many of the earliest church fathers believed that the angels might have been created before the corporeal world, St. Augustine reasoned that the most likely moment of creation for the angels was on the first day when light was created. Medieval theologians, such as St. Bonaventure and St. Thomas Aquinas likewise associated the creation of the angels with God's activity on the first day of creation.

At other times angels are designated as "the holy ones." The psalmist writes, "The heavens praise your marvels, LORD, / your loyalty in the assembly of the holy ones. / Who in the skies ranks with the LORD? / Who is like the LORD among the sons of the gods? / A God dreaded in the council of the holy ones, / greater and more awesome than all those around him!" (Ps 89:6-8). In the book of Daniel,

"watchers" is a way to name angels: "In the vision I saw while in bed, a holy watcher came down from heaven" (4:10). Angels are even identified as "gods." In Psalm 82:1 we read: "God takes a stand in the divine council, / gives judgment in the midst of the gods."

The most common word to designate an angel is "messenger." The Hebrew word for messenger is *malak*. The Greek equivalent (used in the New Testament) is *aggelos* from which we derive the English word "angel." This word tells us that angels are frequently God's messengers.

Although they are often messengers, angels can carry out many other ministries as well. In fact, it is by examining the ministries of angels that we will understand them most effectively. Since we cannot grasp the *spiritual essence* of angels, appreciating their *ministry* or *function* is the best way to discover their importance to us.

The different ministries of angels will be used to organize this study. Each lesson will center on a particular ministry that the Bible tells us angels perform. In addition to learning about each ministry, we will reflect on how these angelic ministries illuminate aspects of our relationship with God (see *Contemporary Relevance* sections throughout our study). Before we proceed, however, we must address a peculiarity that characterizes some of the most ancient biblical passages concerning angels. In these passages there is a dramatic shift in characters. A being who is first presented as an angel suddenly becomes God's own self. We will name this literary phenomenon "slippage," because without warning, an angelic presence "slips" into the presence of God.

Is It an Angel or Is It God?

The Bible is filled with stories describing God's saving action. Beneath all these accounts is the conviction that God seeks a relationship with a people and intends to bring them to fullness of life. Whether the account is about the liberation of Israel from bondage in Egypt or the resurrection of Jesus, the story presumes a connection between God and the creatures God has made. God establishes and supports this connection by interacting with humans.

There are many Scripture passages in which God interacts with humans directly. In the book of Genesis, God walks and talks with Adam and Eve in the garden at the breezy time of day (Gen 3:8). But most of the time, God is depicted as speaking to humans through an intermediary, a messenger or angel. Surprisingly, in some of these passages the distinction between God and God's messenger is blurred. A character who first appears as an angel "slips" into a character who is clearly God.

In Judges 6:11-24, an angel appears to Gideon as he beats out wheat in the wine press. The two begin to talk, and Gideon expresses his sorrow that the Lord has forgotten his people. Then, without any preparation, verse 14 states, "The Lord turned to him and said: Go with the strength you have, and save Israel from the power of Midian. Is it not I who send you?" The person speaking to Gideon, who was introduced as a "messenger of the Lord" (v. 12), has suddenly become "the Lord" in person. The character of an angel has "slipped" into the God of Israel.

Another example of this "slippage" occurs in Genesis 16. Hagar, the slave girl of Sarai, runs away from her mistress because of harsh treatment. She carries a son in her womb. As Hagar wanders in the wilderness, an angel of the Lord finds her by a spring of water. The text calls her visitor "the Lord's angel" four times (vv. 7, 9, 10, and 11). Yet when the angel speaks to Hagar in verse 10, the words sound like the first-person speech of God: "I will make your descendants so numerous . . . that they will be too many to count." After the visitor leaves, Hagar does not believe that she has encountered a messenger. The narrator tells us, "To the Lord who spoke to her she gave a name, saying, 'You are God who sees me'; she meant, 'Have I really seen God and remained alive after he saw me?'" (16:13).

There are other biblical passages that demonstrate a "slippage" between the presence of a messenger and the presence of God. We see this phenomenon when Hagar and her son are saved after his birth (Gen 21:15-21), when Abram is prevented from slaying his son (Gen 22:11-12), when Jacob dreams about sheep (Gen 31:11-13), and when Moses encounters the burning bush (Exod 3:2-6).

What are we to make of these scenes in which the identities of God and God's angel are interchanged? We can approach this question from both a historical and a spiritual perspective. Historically, these passages of "slippage" may have arisen as Israel began to move away from presenting God in direct communication with humans. The ease with which God speaks directly to Adam, Eve, and Noah was gradually replaced by God communicating to humans through intermediaries. Instead of speaking face to face, God sends a messenger or angel to deliver the divine message. In the later books of the Old Testament, God speaks almost exclusively through messengers. But such an approach is a development. Historically, the passages of "slippage" we have identified represent a transition phase in which the use of intermediaries is only partially realized. This is why in these scenes there is almost no interest in the messengers themselves. Angels are minimally described, and they are not given names. The significance of the messenger is solely the message itself. Thus *an angel* giving God's message can suddenly become *God* giving the message. Angels, at this stage, are a personal expression of God's word.

The passages of "slippage" that we have seen can also be viewed from a spiritual perspective. From this standpoint we view them not merely as a stage in a historical development but as an abiding characteristic of our relationship with God. None of us can speak to God face to face. Our relationship is always mediated through created realities. Whether it is through an angel, another human, an experience of nature, or the impact of a significant event, our contact with God is indirect. Yet even as we experience the created reality, God is there. We "slip" from the mediation into the presence of the Creator, and that presence is real. We never see God *directly*, but *we do see God*—in the face of a stranger, the support of a friend, the magnificence of a sunset. Much like the experience of Gideon or Hagar, we think that we are simply doing our work or coping with life's problems, and suddenly we are in the presence of the Almighty. "Divine slippage" does not only occur in the Bible. It also takes place in our lives.

Let us now closely examine two biblical passages in which this "slippage" is present and draw from them insights into our own encounters with God.

Abraham's Visitors

Genesis 18:1-15

Abraham's Visitors. [1]The LORD appeared to Abraham by the oak of Mamre, as he sat in the entrance of his tent, while the day was growing hot. [2]Looking up, he saw three men standing near him. When he saw them, he ran from the entrance of the tent to greet them; and bowing to the ground, [3]he said: "Sir, if it please you, do not go on past your servant. [4]Let some water be brought, that you may bathe your feet, and then rest under the tree. [5]Now that you have come to your servant, let me bring you a little food, that you may refresh yourselves; and afterward you may go on your way." "Very well," they replied, "do as you have said."

[6]Abraham hurried into the tent to Sarah and said, "Quick, three measures of bran flour! Knead it and make bread." [7]He ran to the herd, picked out a tender, choice calf, and gave it to a servant, who quickly prepared it. [8]Then he got some curds and milk, as well as the calf that had been prepared, and set these before them, waiting on them under the tree while they ate.

[9]"Where is your wife Sarah?" they asked him. "There in the tent," he replied. [10]One of them said, "I will return to you about this time next year, and Sarah will then have a son." Sarah was listening at the entrance of the tent, just behind him. [11]Now Abraham and Sarah were old, advanced in years, and Sarah had stopped having her menstrual periods. [12]So Sarah laughed to herself and said, "Now that I am worn out and my husband is old, am I still to have sexual pleasure?" [13]But the LORD said to Abraham: "Why did Sarah laugh and say, 'Will I really bear a child, old as I am?' [14]Is anything too marvelous for the LORD to do? At the appointed time, about this time next year, I will return to you, and Sarah will have a son." [15]Sarah lied, saying, "I did not laugh," because she was afraid. But he said, "Yes, you did."

Chapter 18:1-15 is a pivotal scene in the book of Genesis. It is the final and definitive promise that Abraham and Sarah will have a son. Six chapters earlier, in Genesis 12, God had promised Abraham that he would be the father of a great nation. Yet Sarah remained barren. By chapter 18, both Abraham and Sarah are advanced in age, and Sarah's menstrual cycle has ceased. From every perspective it seems that the promise of offspring can no longer be fulfilled. It is in this barren and hopeless condition that God speaks to Abraham.

This scene clearly demonstrates the "slippage" between God and God's messengers that we have seen in other biblical passages. The first verse informs us that God is about to appear to Abraham by the oak of Mamre. But the manner of God's appearance is confusing at best. When Abraham looks up, he sees three men. The text does not refer to these men as angels or messengers. They appear only as three men standing before Abraham as the day is growing hot. We have been told that it is God who appears to Abraham, but how are we to understand this unexpected manifestation? Should we understand God to be one of the men, while the other two men are angels? Is God appearing under the guise of three men? Are all three men angels commissioned to speak for God? Is this an early anticipation of God as Trinity? All of these possibilities have been suggested. What is clear is that the text insists that God comes to Abraham not directly but in a mediated form.

Scripture commentators have long debated the identity and roles of the **three angels sent to Abraham** in Genesis 18. St. Augustine (4th century) was the first exegete to suggest a foreshadowing of the doctrine of the Trinity in this mysterious visit, offering the following spiritual interpretation: "[S]ince three men appeared, and no one of them is said to be greater than the rest either in form, or age, or power, why should we not here understand, as visibly intimated by the visible creature, the equality of the Trinity, and one and the same substance in three persons" (*On the Trinity*, II.11, in James Kugel, *Traditions of the Bible* [Cambridge, MA: Harvard University Press, 1998], 342).

The mediation of three men is particularly elusive, especially when we consider how Abraham speaks to his visitors. Although we would expect Abraham to address these three men in the plural, he frequently speaks to them in the singular. In the original Hebrew, the plural is used in verses 2 and 4-9. But in verses 3 and 10, the grammar indicates Abraham is speaking to one person rather than multiple people. By verses 13-15 it becomes clear that Abraham is having a conversation with God alone. The fluctuation in the mode of Abraham's speech heightens the "slippage" between the three men and God.

Contemporary Relevance: This powerful passage presents us with a God who brings life and hope to a couple awash in barrenness. What insights can we draw from this story that can illuminate our own encounters with God? The depth and richness of the story generate many possibilities:

1) *Our meetings with God often come unexpectedly.* The three men suddenly appear to Abraham. He does not see them approaching over the desert sands. As he sits at the entrance of his tent, he simply looks up and they are there, standing near him. As much as we may plan or anticipate God's arrival, God does not follow our schedule. We might expect God to speak to us at church or during private prayer. But God is just as likely to meet us at the supermarket, on the soccer field, or as we doze on the backyard patio. God's presence occurs at God's initiative. Our role is not to coax or direct it, but to wait for it with hope and to recognize it when it appears.

2) *God comes to the hospitable.* Although we cannot predict God's arrival, those who serve others are most likely to encounter God. When Abraham sees the three men, he immediately swings into action. He offers them hospitality, bathing their feet and feeding them with bread, milk, and meat. There is no indication that Abraham recognizes anything special about these visitors. They are simply strangers to welcome. The first eight verses of this scene are taken up with the hospitality of Abraham. It is only after his guests have eaten that their real purpose is revealed. Without explanation, they know of Sarah's barrenness. They promise a son. This story tells us that the best context to meet God is in service to others. Whether it is welcoming strangers, feeding the hungry, or caring for the poor, God emerges through acts of hospitality. Like Abraham, when we care for others, we discover that we have welcomed both angels and God's own self.

3) *Nothing is too marvelous for God.* This story purposely unfolds in an impossible situation. A woman after menopause is not able to bear children. Both Abraham and Sarah know this and are resigned to it. Yet God appears and tells them they will have a son. God promises the impossible. God can do this because nothing is impossible for God. The text offers this truth in the form of a question: "Is anything too marvelous for the LORD to do?" (v. 14). The question demands a response. Do Abraham and Sarah believe it? Do *we* believe it?

This question is posed to us. Indeed it is the fundamental question of faith. Do we believe that God has the power to bring about every good thing for us and for our world? Can we accept that God is not limited by our limitations? Do we believe that God can bring life into a barren womb, a barren heart, a barren world? If not, our faith is at odds with the God of the Scriptures, and we may have missed the angels that God has sent to us.

Although God's power over the impossible is foundational to faith, the Bible is not naïve in its application. God can do the impossible, but the Scriptures recognize that God is not bound to do what we desire. Jesus himself experienced this. In the garden before his death he prayed that the cup of suffering might pass him by: "Abba, Father, all things are possible to you. Take this cup away from me, but not what I will but what you will" (Mark 14:36). As we know, Jesus' cup of suffering was not removed. God can do all things, but God does not choose to do all things. The power of God does not provide us with a magical escape from the human condition.

The story of Abraham and Sarah tells us that when God chooses to act, God is free—free from the limits we place upon the possible. Unaccountable to our science and logic, God can bring life to places where life seems impossible. God is not constrained by what we understand or expect. God will not be limited to what we can imagine. Nothing is too wonderful for the Lord to do.

4) *God does not need our faith.* Perhaps the most profound truth of this story is that God's action is not dependent on our cooperation. Although God invites us to believe, our lack of response does not impede God's will.

This truth is presented in Genesis with exquisite artistry. God is shown as the one who initiates the good news. God announces to Abraham that this time next year he will have a son (v. 10). As we have seen, such a promise is a wondrous impossibility. Nevertheless, God intends to bring it about. How do Abraham and Sarah react to God's words? Not well! Their response is deficient. There is no response from Abraham. Having been told that he will be a father, he is silent. He demonstrates no acceptance, rejection, or gratitude for the promise. Perhaps he is simply unable to take the wondrous message in.

It is Sarah who responds for both of them. Hearing God's words as she listens by the entrance of the tent, Sarah laughs (v. 12). The laugh is an expression of doubt. How could such an impossible promise be taken seriously? Yet laughter is not an outright rejection of God's plan. It imagines the beauty of the possibility even as it questions it. The fact that Sarah envisions renewed sexual pleasure with her husband only highlights the ecstasy that she is entertaining. "A son," she thinks, "the desire of my life, the lifting of my barrenness, the fulfillment of our love. It is wonderful. It is doubtful. It is laughable!"

The laughter of Sarah does not frustrate God's plan. The divine visitor hears it even though Sarah is out of sight. He does not criticize the laugh nor reject Sarah. He simply repeats the promise to Abraham: "I will return to you, and Sarah will have a son" (v. 14). When Sarah tries to deny the laugh, the visitor dismisses her attempt. The promise has been made, and it has been laughed at. The promise has been made, and Abraham and Sarah cannot accept it. The laughter of Sarah ends the story, but the reader knows there is more to come. Even though Abraham and Sarah have failed to believe, God is committed to the promise. In a year, a son will be born. The impossible will take place. On that day Abraham and Sarah will truly have something to laugh about (Gen 21:6).

In the face of human doubt, God is faithful. God's purpose is not deterred by our failure to believe. We have all had times in our lives when we have doubted God's promises. As a marriage ends in divorce, the promise of healing seems impossible. With the diagnosis of cancer, courage and hope may seem out of reach. At the death of a child, parents wonder whether life can continue. In such circumstances, the story of Abraham's visitors should give us comfort. We are not the first to doubt God's power or fail to recognize the presence of angels. The challenge to believe in life in the midst of barrenness remains. Sarah's doubt is ours as well. But as in the case of Sarah, God's good purposes are not affected by our lack of faith. Whether we believe or not, the promise stands. Our God is determined to change barrenness into life, doubt into grace, and hopelessness into joy.

Jacob at the Jabbok River

Genesis 32:23-33

Jacob's New Name. ²³That night, however, Jacob arose, took his two wives, with the two maidservants and his eleven children, and crossed the ford of the Jabbok. ²⁴After he got them and brought them across the wadi and brought over what belonged to him, ²⁵Jacob was left there alone. Then a man wrestled with him until the break of dawn. ²⁶When the man saw that he could not prevail over him, he struck Jacob's hip at its socket, so that Jacob's socket was dislocated as he wrestled with him. ²⁷The man then said, "Let me go, for it is daybreak." But Jacob said, "I will not let you go until you bless me." ²⁸"What is your name?" the man asked. He answered, "Jacob." ²⁹Then the man said, "You shall no longer be named Jacob, but Israel, because you have contended with divine and human beings and have prevailed." ³⁰Jacob then asked him, "Please tell me your name." He answered, "Why do you ask for my name?" With that, he blessed him. ³¹Jacob named the place Peniel, "because I have seen God face to face," he said, "yet my life has been spared."

³²At sunrise, as he left Penuel, Jacob limped along because of his hip. ³³That is why, to this day, the Israelites do not eat the sciatic muscle that is on the hip socket, because he had struck Jacob's hip socket at the sciatic muscle.

"Slippage" in the encounter with the divine is amply demonstrated in Jacob's experience at the ford of the Jabbok. After leading his family and goods across the river, Jacob finds himself alone at night. Without any preparation, "a man" appears. There is no further description of this man, but his purpose is clear: he is to fight with Jacob. The fight is neither casual nor brief. It lasts until daybreak! The identity of this unnamed stranger is covered in mystery. But as the narrative continues, it becomes clear that Jacob has encountered some heavenly being. He presses to know the man's name because in the ancient world a name was not a mere tag or identity marker but a revelation of a being's nature. Jacob wants to know what kind of being opposes him. He asks for a blessing because he intuits that this stranger has divine power.

The medieval Jewish scholar Maimonides identified elements of a prophetic vision in the account of **Jacob's wrestling match at the ford of Jabbok**. Such visions, often mediated by angels, are the way God frequently inspires prophets in the Old Testament. The revelation made to Jacob in Genesis 32:23-33 is conveyed by means of the granting of a new name: Jacob becomes Israel (meaning "he contends" or "he struggles"), for he has "contended with divine and human beings and . . . prevailed" (32:29). In this prophetic renaming, Jacob—and by extension his descendants—receive divine assurance that they will be victorious in their future struggles.

Interpreters of this passage frequently suggest that the man who contends with Jacob is an angel. Some rabbis went so far as to suggest that the angel asks to leave before dawn so that he can join in the morning choir before God's throne. This passage, then, is often titled "Jacob's Struggle with an Angel." Yet by verse 31 it becomes clear that Jacob's opponent is God. As Jacob realizes, "I have seen God face to face . . . yet my life has been spared."

Contemporary Relevance: The ambiguity of this story is not limited to the identity of the stranger who appears to Jacob. The lack of clarity permeates the narrative. But it also opens new possibilities to understand our relationship with God. This story suggests that we sometimes encounter God in uncomfortable ways. Although we routinely perceive ourselves as listening to God, speaking with God, and even arguing with God, this passage suggests that sometimes we even wrestle with God. There are times when the injustice of our world or the unfairness of our lives overcomes us. We call out to God for answers, guidance, and wisdom. But there is no response. In such times God may appear to us not as a friend but as an assailant, a silent stranger with whom we must fight.

The most remarkable aspect of this story is that the fight is presented as one between equals. At times Jacob has the upper hand. The stranger cannot prevail over him and asks Jacob to let him go. Yet the stranger has his own strength and resources. He strikes a serious blow to Jacob's hip at its socket and will not reveal to Jacob his name. Although verse 29 says that Jacob has prevailed over divine and human beings, such a statement must be seen as an exaggeration. It is better to claim that the wrestling match ends in a draw. God is still God. The stranger leaves the struggle without revealing his name. Jacob is still Jacob, but he is changed. He has a new name, Israel. He leaves both wounded and blessed.

This narrative reveals to us a God who is willing to meet us on our own level. Although transcendent and totally other, God condescends not only to meet with us but to brawl with us. Our God receives the strikes of our anger as we assert that God is silent and does not care. Our God absorbs our complaints that we have been dealt with unfairly and that God does not deserve our love. As mistaken as such attitudes may be, God accepts them because God accepts us. God understands that our perception is limited and is willing to accept our blows so that our vision can ultimately be enlarged.

Nor is God's condescension a hollow gesture. God invites us to battle over the things we feel and believe. God has made us creatures with emotion and intellect. Our feelings can be extreme. Our thinking can be misguided. But God embraces us as we are, balanced or unhinged, perceptive or confused, faith-filled or overwhelmed with doubt. God is willing to speak with us. God is also willing to fight with us!

When we contend with God's angels or God's own self, most fights end in a draw. God never uses power to force a victory. But neither do we leave the battle victorious. We usually end our struggle with God without the answers we desire or the explanations we demand. And sometimes, like Jacob, we walk away with a limp. We are wounded in the knowledge that we are only human and will never fully understand God's ways. Yet we are not defined by woundedness alone. A combat with the Holy One is also a blessing. When we contend with God, our struggle itself confirms that our relationship with God is real. Those without faith ignore God. Only those who on some level believe have the desire to wrestle God. Even when the fight does not produce a winner, we are blessed to have encountered the God who accepts us as we are and absorbs our attacks. Only love can explain why the Lord of the Universe is willing to wrestle with us until the break of dawn.

From "Slippage" to Insight

The narratives of the Bible are our access to the reality of angels. Yet these narratives do not present angels to us in any organized or consistent way. The diversity of terms that can identify an angel testifies to the time and development that were necessary for the belief in angels to evolve. A remarkable number of stories demonstrate a "slippage" of identity between God and God's messengers. Scenes which begin with an account between a person and God's messenger can slip into an account between a person and God's own self. Although interpreters of such narratives can be frustrated to find such ambiguity, the ease with which angels and God replace each other leads to an important theological insight: angels often do what God does. In the Bible, God can communicate with humans directly, but God can also send an angel. God and angels deal with us in similar ways.

The biblical narratives we will examine in the upcoming lessons will show less "slippage" between angels and God. The presentation of angels will become more differentiated and stable. Angels will emerge as distinct creatures of God, sometimes with a personal name. Yet even with this development, angels will continue to do what God does. Their ministry is to represent God's own will and action in our world. It is through that ministry that angels are best understood.

We will use the ministries of angels to organize the next five lessons of this study. We will examine angels as they worship the holy, speak for God, rule the cosmos, destroy evil, and protect God's own. These actions are also God's actions. Angels are one means of God achieving God's purposes. As we examine the ministries of angels, we will be examining the work of God. This is why it is possible to say that in studying angels we are studying God.

EXPLORING LESSON ONE

1. Why does this lesson assert that we cannot investigate angels themselves? If angels cannot be examined directly, how can we learn about them?

_____

_____

_____

_____

_____

2. Christian belief in angels has its roots in Judaism. What significance do you find in the fact that angels appear in both the Old and New Testaments and are a part of both the Jewish and Christian faiths?

_____

_____

_____

_____

_____

3. What are some different names used to describe or designate angels in the Bible? Do any of these names deepen your appreciation of angels?

_____

_____

_____

_____

4. "Slippage" describes the dynamic relationship between God and God's angels found in several Old Testament passages (Gen 16:7-13; 18:1-15; 32:23-33; Judg 6:11-24). What are some common characteristics shared by passages in which "slippage" occurs?

_____

_____

_____

_____

_____

5. The story of Abraham's visitors offers an example of "slippage" and reminds us that we can find ourselves suddenly and unexpectedly in God's presence (Gen 18:1-15). Recall an occasion of "divine slippage" in your own life—a time when you found yourself suddenly in the presence of God.

_____

_____

_____

_____

_____

6. Abraham encountered God in the midst of hospitality to strangers. What role do you think hospitality plays in the Christian life?

_____

_____

_____

_____

_____

7. In response to Abraham and Sarah's skepticism that they will have a son in their old age, God asks Abraham a fundamental question: "Is anything too marvelous for the LORD to do?" (Gen 18:14). In what situations might God be asking you this question? How might you respond?

_____

_____

_____

_____

_____

8. a) After struggling with God, Jacob leaves with a limp and a blessing (Gen 32:30, 32). How would you explain the spiritual concept of "wrestling with God"?

_____

_____

_____

_____

b) As you look back on your own struggles with God, are there ways in which you were damaged by them? Are there ways in which you were blessed through them?

_____

_____

_____

_____

9. What is something that you learned in this lesson that was especially interesting or meaningful to you?

_____

_____

_____

_____

_____

_____

CLOSING PRAYER

Prayer

But the LORD said to Abraham, "Why did Sarah laugh and say, 'Will I really bear a child, old as I am?' Is anything too marvelous for the LORD to do?" (Gen 18:13-14a)

Eternal God, your power is not limited by what our finite minds can imagine or our doubting hearts can believe. Grant us the grace to place our trust in you and the wisdom to accept your will in all things. We especially pray today for . . .

LESSON TWO

Worshiping the Holy:
Angels Before God's Throne

Begin your personal study and group discussion with a simple and sincere prayer such as:

Prayer

God of heaven and earth, may our time of study and reflection lead us to imitate the angels as heralds of your word and proclaimers of your glory.

Read pages 26–34, Lesson Two.

Respond to the questions on pages 35–37, Exploring Lesson Two.

The Closing Prayer on page 38 is for your personal use and may be used at the end of group discussion.

WORSHIPING THE HOLY: ANGELS BEFORE GOD'S THRONE

We usually think of angels in relation to ourselves. We are eager to understand how angels connect us to the divine, speak to us on behalf of God, and guide us in God's ways. Yet the highest and most fundamental function of angels does not involve us at all. Angels' primary ministry is to praise God. They extol God's goodness and exalt God's holiness. We are right, therefore, to envision angels around God's heavenly throne, singing God's praises without end. In this lesson we will explore the diverse ways the Bible presents angels in their principal ministry of worshiping God.

 St. Basil, a father of the church who lived in the fourth century, noted that while it is the special ministry of the angels to glorify God, **praising the Creator** is the universal duty of every creature, "whether it speaks or is silent, whether in heaven or on earth" (*On Prayer*, in M. F. Toal, *The Sunday Sermons of the Great Fathers*, vol. II [London: Longmans, 1958], 385–86).

The ministry of worship is connected to the biblical concept of the heavenly court. As the writers of the Hebrew Scriptures searched for ways to present God's power, they drew upon the practices of earthly kings. The rulers of this world were never seen to function in isolation. They were surrounded by servants and ministers who enlarged and promoted their power. They reigned from elaborately decorated thrones surrounded by a royal court, magnificently attired. The biblical authors, then, imagined that God also had a heavenly council. God's council was similar to those of earthly rulers, but it was infinitely greater and more glorious. An explicit description of this divine court is given in 1 Kings 22:19b-22. The prophet Micaiah reports a vision to the king of Israel:

[19b]"I saw the Lord seated on his throne, with the whole host of heaven standing to his right and to his left. [20]The Lord asked: Who will deceive Ahab, so that he will go up and fall on Ramoth-gilead? And one said this, another that, [21]until this spirit came forth and stood before the Lord, saying, 'I will deceive him.' The Lord asked: How? [22]He answered, 'I will go forth and become a lying spirit in the mouths of all his prophets.' The Lord replied: You shall succeed in deceiving him. Go forth and do this."

In Micaiah's vision, God is seated on a throne with the host of heaven standing to the right and left. When a decision must be made on how to deceive King Ahab, God opens a discussion among the assembled ministers. After debate, one spirit makes a suggestion that Ahab can be deceived by the spirit misleading Ahab's own prophets. God accepts this suggestion and sends the spirit to act accordingly.

The psalms also envision God situated in the midst of a council. Psalm 82:1 reads: "God takes a stand in the divine council, / gives judgment in the midst of the gods" and Psalm 89:6-8 declares:

[6]The heavens praise your marvels, Lord,
　your loyalty in the assembly of the holy ones.
[7]Who in the skies ranks with the Lord?
　Who is like the Lord among the sons of the gods?

[8]A God dreaded in the council of the holy ones,
greater and more awesome than all those
around him!

In the book of Job, Eliphaz pictures God in the royal court: "Do you listen in on God's council / and restrict wisdom to yourself?" (Job 15:8). Jeremiah also speaks of God's council: "Now, who has stood in the council of the Lord, / to see him and to hear his word?" (Jer 23:18).

In addition to having a council, earthly kings also have armies, so the Bible presumes that God has such resources as well. When Joshua is preparing for battle, he raises his eyes and sees "one who stood facing him, drawn sword in hand." Joshua asks, "Are you one of us or one of our enemies?" The one with the drawn sword replies, "Neither. I am the commander of the army of the Lord: now I have come" (Josh 5:13-14).

The appearance of the **heavenly "commander"** in Joshua 5:13-14 is the fulfillment of a promise, made by God to Moses, that he will send his angel before the Israelites when they enter the Promised Land. Armed with God's own "authority" this angel's mission will be to protect the Israelites on their way and destroy whatever enemies they might encounter in Canaan (Exod 23:20-23).

Another example of a divine army can be found in 2 Kings when Elisha's servant despairs over the number of enemy troops facing them in battle. Elisha opens his servant's eyes to see that the mountainside was filled with fiery chariots and horses around Elisha (2 Kgs 6:17). This is God's army. These heavenly beings are envisioned as a host of fighters. They give rise to a familiar title for God: "The Lord of hosts" (e.g., 1 Sam 1:3; Ps 24:10; Isa 6:3). Although this name for God originated as a military term, its meaning broadened through time. The title is used most frequently by the prophets (247 out of 285 occurrences). In their usage the title surpasses any comparison to a human court or army. The Lord of hosts is the one God of heaven and earth. This God alone is worshiped by angels. It is in the performance of this ministry of praise that we receive the most detailed description of angels in the Bible.

The Cherubim

Ezekiel 1:1-28

The Vision: God on the Cherubim. [1]In the thirtieth year, on the fifth day of the fourth month, while I was among the exiles by the river Chebar, the heavens opened, and I saw divine visions.— [2]On the fifth day of the month—this was the fifth year of King Jehoiachin's exile— [3]the word of the Lord came to the priest Ezekiel, the son of Buzi, in the land of the Chaldeans by the river Chebar. There the hand of the Lord came upon him.

[4]As I watched, a great stormwind came from the North, a large cloud with flashing fire, a bright glow all around it, and something like polished metal gleamed at the center of the fire. [5]From within it figures in the likeness of four living creatures appeared. This is what they looked like: [6]They were in human form, but each had four faces and four wings, [7]and their legs were straight, the soles of their feet like the hooves of a bull, gleaming like polished brass. [8]Human hands were under their wings, and the wings of one touched those of another. [9]Their faces and their wings looked out on all their four sides; they did not turn when they moved, but each went straight ahead.

[10]Their faces were like this: each of the four had a human face, and on the right the face of a lion, and on the left, the face of an ox, and each had the face of an eagle. [11]Such were their faces. Their wings were spread out above. On each one, two wings touched one another, and the other two wings covered the body. [12]Each went straight

continue

ahead. Wherever the spirit would go, they went; they did not change direction when they moved. [13]And the appearance of the living creatures seemed like burning coals of fire. Something indeed like torches moved back and forth among the living creatures. The fire gleamed intensely, and from it lightning flashed. [14]The creatures darting back and forth flashed like lightning.

[15]As I looked at the living creatures, I saw wheels on the ground, one alongside each of the four living creatures. [16]The wheels and their construction sparkled like yellow topaz, and all four of them looked the same: their construction seemed as though one wheel was inside the other. [17]When they moved, they went in any of the four directions without veering as they moved. [18]The four of them had rims, high and fearsome—eyes filled the four rims all around. [19]When the living creatures moved, the wheels moved with them; and when the living creatures were raised from the ground, the wheels also were raised. [20]Wherever the spirit would go, they went. And they were raised up together with the living creatures, for the spirit of the living creatures was in the wheels. [21]Wherever the living creatures moved, the wheels moved; when they stood still, the wheels stood still. When they were lifted up from the earth, the wheels were lifted up with them. For the spirit of the living creatures was in the wheels.

[22]Above the heads of the living creatures was a likeness of the firmament; it was awesome, stretching upwards like shining crystal over their heads. [23]Beneath the firmament their wings stretched out toward one another; each had two wings covering the body. [24]Then I heard the sound of their wings, like the roaring of mighty waters, like the voice of the Almighty. When they moved, the sound of the tumult was like the din of an army. And when they stood still, they lowered their wings. [25]While they stood with their wings lowered, a voice came from above the firmament over their heads.

[26]Above the firmament over their heads was the likeness of a throne that looked like sapphire; and upon this likeness of a throne was seated, up above, a figure that looked like a human being.

[27]And I saw something like polished metal, like the appearance of fire enclosed on all sides, from what looked like the waist up; and from what looked like the waist down, I saw something like the appearance of fire and brilliant light surrounding him. [28]Just like the appearance of the rainbow in the clouds on a rainy day so was the appearance of brilliance that surrounded him. Such was the appearance of the likeness of the glory of the LORD. And when I saw it, I fell on my face and heard a voice speak.

The most vivid and forceful description of God's heavenly court occurs in this passage from the book of Ezekiel. Here we encounter a deluge of imagery that overwhelms us.

What is essential in this lengthy passage is that Ezekiel is seeing a revelation of God's glory. After a brief *introduction (vv. 1-3)* which situates Ezekiel at the Chebar river in exile, the vision unfolds in three phases: the sight of *the living creatures (vv. 4-14), the wheels (vv. 15-21), and the firmament and the throne (vv. 22-27)*. A one-verse *conclusion (v. 28)* provides Ezekiel's reaction to the vision.

Ezekiel does not at first realize he is witnessing a manifestation of God. The vision unfolds in stages. First the prophet only sees a large luminous cloud coming with the "storm-wind" from the north. But the cloud is an initial clue that God's presence is about to be revealed: God came to Moses in a cloud on Mt. Sinai (Exod 19:9), and a "column of cloud" stood at the entrance to the meeting tent, when God spoke to Moses face to face (Exod 33:9). In the cloud that Ezekiel sees, there is flashing fire, and in the midst of the fire "something like polished metal" (v. 4). The Hebrew word that our translation renders "polished metal" carries the sense of a bright substance, the color of fire. This is Ezekiel's unique way to describe God's glory. But the prophet does not yet recognize it for what it is. At this point, Ezekiel notices four living creatures in the lower part of the cloud. A wheel covered with eyes then becomes visible beneath each creature. Finally,

Ezekiel sees above the creatures a sapphire throne on which a shining, human-like figure sits, encased by the brilliance of a rainbow. Only then does the prophet realize he is seeing the glory of God. He falls to the ground in awe.

The vision of Ezekiel is a human attempt to describe the heavenly court of God. But where are the angels? They are present, though this is not immediately apparent. We find them beneath God's throne: they are the living creatures that Ezekiel sees in the cloud. Later in the book, Ezekiel uses another term to identify these creatures, helping us make the connection to angels. The term is "cherubim" (10:1-2, 20). "Cherubim" is the plural of "cherub." The Hebrew word for cherub/cherubim occurs ninety-one times in the Old Testament. The etymology of "cherub" indicates that the word means "to bless or worship." This root meaning renders the term appropriate for created beings of the heavenly court whose function is to worship God.

 Cherubim are appointed "to guard the way to the tree of life" after the expulsion of Adam and Eve from Eden (Gen 3:24). Their function as guards in this account from Genesis echoes similar accounts of supernatural beings in Babylonian mythology who guarded royal palaces and temple gates.

The four living creatures of Ezekiel's vision, then, are cherubim. Their appearance is dauntingly confusing! They are like humans in their erect posture, hands, and legs. Yet they are unlike humans because they have hooved feet, four faces, and four wings. They seem arranged in a square configuration with the tips of their wings touching each other. Their four faces are described carefully. Each cherub has the face of a lion, an eagle, an ox, and a human. As we discussed in Lesson One, angels do not actually look the way they are described in the Bible. The description in Ezekiel, therefore, is a human effort to describe spiritual beings who

are without material form. But why does Ezekiel use such bizarre images to describe God's ministers? Why are the cherubim presented as a mixture of human and animal forms?

The hybrid living creatures of Ezekiel are symbols derived from the throne rooms of earthly kings in the ancient Near East. Fantastic hybrid creatures were often part of royal art. The rulers of Syria and Mesopotamia apparently requested depictions of animals with human heads or humans with animal heads and feet to decorate their court and display the immensity of their power. Colossal composite figures were created to guard the doorways of royal palaces. The king's throne was the most likely place to display these creatures. In archaeological remains, royal thrones are often carved with winged sphinxes or lions with human heads. This best explains why the living creatures of Ezekiel's vision are located below God (v. 26). The cherubim form God's throne; they support God's majesty and power.

This positioning is confirmed by the biblical assertion that God "sits upon the cherubim." 1 Samuel 4:4 states that the Lord was recognized as the one who is "enthroned upon the cherubim." The directions for Solomon's temple prescribed that two cherubim made of olive wood and overlaid with gold should occupy the holy of holies. Their outstretched wings should touch each other and extend over the ark of the covenant. Their wings formed the throne from which God was understood to rule (1 Kgs 6:23-28).

Ezekiel's vision specifically describes the four faces of the cherubim (v. 10). What is their significance? The lion is recognized for its strength. The love between David and Jonathan was described as "stronger than lions" (2 Sam 1:23). The eagle is seen as the swiftest of birds. Lamentations 4:19 describes Israel's enemies as swifter "than eagles in the sky." The bull is the most valued domestic animal. Proverbs 14:4 says, "Where there are no oxen, the crib is clean; / but abundant crops come through the strength of the bull." Human beings are the height of creation. They are made in God's image (Gen 1:27) and are called to rule creation (Ps 8:7). Therefore, the four faces of Ezekiel's cherubim effectively summarize the greatness of creation, representing all that God has made. They also reflect God's majesty, which is as powerful as a lion, as free as an eagle, as generative as an ox, and as wise as a human. In addition, the number four recalls the "four corners of the earth" (Isa 11:12). The four cherubim, therefore, emphasize that God's majesty extends to the whole world. The cherubim who support God's throne signify the nature and scope of God's power.

Contemporary Relevance: Two valuable and relevant truths can be drawn from this passage. The first concerns the transcendence of God. In our time it is common to understand God as a loving Father or as a friend who accompanies us through life. Such images are both biblical and true, and we should treasure them. Yet in our efforts to describe God's closeness and love, we should not reduce God to the commonplace. God is close to us, but God is not like us. God's love for us is not like any other love we have known. The vision of Ezekiel is bizarre and confusing—intentionally so. The multiplicity of images that bend our minds as we attempt to visualize them emphasize the otherness of the divine. We are meant to see something wonderful but not anything we can completely understand or control. By pushing the images of the cherubim to the extreme, this vision asserts that no representation of God's throne can be accurate. God is beyond any verbal or visual description. God is other and beyond all created things.

Although God's power is reflected in the four cherubim, God is not identified with them. This is why God is pictured as separated from the cherubim by a "firmament" that acts as a platform on which God sits (v. 22). This keeps God distinct from creation. It is also why the four living creatures cover their bodies with their second pair of wings (v. 11). Like Ezekiel who falls on his face when he realizes what he is seeing, the cherubim recognize their unworthiness in the presence of the divine. We too must never presume that we can fully picture or understand God. God's glory surpasses our

imagination. We can never completely grasp God's presence. It is only when we accept God's complete otherness that we can begin to appreciate the wonder of God's desire to form a relationship with us. It is when we recognize that God is transcendent that we can truly marvel at the depth of God's love.

The second truth we can draw from this passage derives from the mobility of God's throne. God "sits upon the cherubim," yet God's throne is not fixed. It is able to move to any part of creation. Not only do the cherubim move by God's spirit, they move without changing direction (v. 12). God's mobility is further emphasized by the wheels that connect to each of the cherubim. The wheels move with the cherubim and are also guided by God's spirit (vv. 19-20). Psalm 18:11 also stresses the mobility of God: "Mounted on a cherub he flew, / borne along on the wings of the wind." God's throne, supported by the cherubim, is moveable. God is free to go wherever divine power is to be shown.

Ezekiel receives his vision in exile. Verses 1-3 clearly situate the prophet on the banks of the river Chebar, which was most likely a canal near Nippur in Babylon. This was one of the sites on which the Jews settled during their exile from their homeland. Receiving a vision in this location is significant. In the ancient Near East, gods were associated with a particular country and located in a distinct temple. When the Jews were forced to leave their homeland and the temple of Solomon was destroyed, it would have been easy for some exiles to conclude that they no longer lived within the scope of God's power. Ezekiel's vision contradicts this assumption. The God of Israel is not limited to a specific place. God rules from a moveable throne. The nature and scope of God's power, reflected in the four cherubim, can extend anywhere. Although the Jews are in exile, God is still present to them.

Any one of us can find ourselves in exile. We can be separated from someone we love by distance or misunderstanding. We can experience the loss of health or diminishment of strength that comes with advancing age. The hope with which we once faced the future can be lost. In such diminished and debilitating conditions, the temptation is to believe that God has been left behind in the good times that once were. Like the Jews of the exile, we might conclude that God is trapped in some distant place or time. The vision of Ezekiel shatters such presumptions. It asserts that our God is not attached to any location. God is not fixed but free! God rides upon the cherubim who move effortlessly in any direction. When we are tempted to despair because we are no longer in the place where God was, this vision encourages us to hope. We do not need to go to God. God comes to us.

The Seraphim

Isaiah 6:1-8

The Sending of Isaiah. ¹In the year King Uzziah died, I saw the Lord seated on a high and lofty throne, with the train of his garment filling the temple. ²Seraphim were stationed above; each of them had six wings: with two they covered their faces, with two they covered their feet, and with two they hovered. ³One cried out to the other:

"Holy, holy, holy is the LORD of hosts!
   All the earth is filled with his glory!"

⁴At the sound of that cry, the frame of the door shook and the house was filled with smoke.

⁵Then I said, "Woe is me, I am doomed! For I am a man of unclean lips, living among a people of unclean lips, and my eyes have seen the King, the LORD of hosts!" ⁶Then one of the seraphim flew to me, holding an ember which he had taken with tongs from the altar.

⁷He touched my mouth with it. "See," he said, "now that this has touched your lips, your wickedness is removed, your sin purged."

⁸Then I heard the voice of the Lord saying, "Whom shall I send? Who will go for us?" "Here I am," I said; "send me!"

Another significant scene of God's heavenly court is found in this passage from the book of Isaiah. As we would expect, angels are present. They are vividly described. Although this vision takes place in the Jerusalem temple, it is in fact a glimpse into the heavenly court of God. Isaiah, in effect, has been admitted into the divine council. He sees God seated on a high and lofty throne. There is no direct description of God. The size of God's garment which alone fills the temple indicates God's greatness (v. 1). The smoke that fills the house is a counterpart to the cloud associated with the divine presence (v. 4). It both reveals and conceals God, preserving God's complete transcendence.

God is not alone in the vision. Spiritual beings called "seraphim" surround the divine throne. Unlike the word for *cherubim*, the word for *seraphim* (which seems to derive from the Hebrew root "to burn") is rare in the Hebrew Scriptures. It occurs only seven times: twice in this passage, twice in Numbers 21:4-9, and once each in Deuteronomy 8:15, Isaiah 14:29, and Isaiah 30:6. Outside of Isaiah 6, the term refers to either poisonous or flying serpents. This makes it likely that Isaiah 6 envisions the seraphim as winged serpents around God's throne.

As surprising as this image may seem to us, Isaiah's audience would not see it as unusual. Serpents, especially the cobra, were routinely associated with the royal court in Egypt. They were seen as protectors of the ruler. The throne of the Pharaoh Tutankhamon (King Tut) has armrests with cobras facing forward with wings and a coiled tail. The back of the throne depicts cobra heads to ward off evil from behind. Egyptian depictions of the pharaoh often show serpents hovering above and behind him. This is precisely where the seraphim are positioned in Isaiah's vision (v. 2). Just as Israel seems to have borrowed from Mesopotamia the composite winged animals as a model for the cherubim in Ezekiel 1, the hovering serpents of Egypt seem to be the pattern for the seraphim in Isaiah 6.

Some scholars have attempted to identify a specific reptile native to the region that might correspond to the winged and burning serpents unleashed by God to punish the Israelites in Numbers 21:6. Such interpretations attribute the name **seraph** (likely meaning "fiery" or "burning") to the inflammation caused by the bite of such a serpent. Other commentators, however, see the seraph serpents as legendary animals similar to those found elsewhere in the Old Testament such as Behemoth and Leviathan (e.g., Job 40:15, 25; Ps 74:14; Isa 27:1). The figure of a seraph that God commanded Moses to make as an antidote to the plague of poisonous serpents was preserved and eventually became an object of veneration in the Jerusalem temple where it was even given a name—Nehushtan. This artifact was destroyed during the religious reforms of King Hezekiah, according to 2 Kings 18:4.

Yet what Israel borrowed it also transformed. The winged serpents of Egypt were present to protect the Pharaoh. In Isaiah's vision the seraphim seem to be protecting themselves. Four of their six wings are used to cover themselves from God's glory. The seraphim's purpose is not to *protect* God but to *praise* God. They cry out to each other: "Holy, holy, holy." Holiness is the essential quality of God, indicating God's otherness, transcendence, and difference from all that is sinful or finite. The sound of the seraphim's cry shakes the temple (v. 4). The God of Israel needs no protection. God receives constant adoration. Like the cherubim in Ezekiel's vison, the ministry of the seraphim is to worship the Almighty. They eternally proclaim God's holiness and glory.

When Isaiah sees this vision of God's court, he cries out, "Woe is me, I am doomed! For I am a man of unclean lips, living among a people of unclean lips" (v. 5). His words are not so much a confession of sin as a recognition of his finite condition. When he sees the truth about God, he recognizes the truth about himself. If God is complete holiness, Isaiah is compromised holiness. If God is ultimate glory, the prophet recognizes his own inherent imperfection. The vision, however, does not end with Isaiah's weakness. One of the seraphim flies to him. The seraph does not move on its own. Everything in God's court is directed by God's will. God sends the angel to change Isaiah, to remove wickedness and sin (v. 6). This change is much more than just the erasure of Isaiah's personal sins and mistakes. It is a transformation of the finite prophet to serve the infinite God. Isaiah is moved close enough to ultimate holiness that he can speak for the Lord of Hosts.

Contemporary Relevance: This text makes it clear that human transformation may at times seem impossible or frightening. A seraph picks up a burning coal from the altar. The heat and destructive nature of the coal is emphasized by the seraph using tongs to carry it (v. 6). If a mighty seraph cannot touch the burning coal, what will happen when the coal touches the prophet's lips? Such contact will certainly burn through Isaiah! Yet no harm to Isaiah is mentioned in the text.

This surprisingly benign result addresses our own fear of transformation. Sometimes we imagine that a change is too difficult to endure, that amending our set patterns will destroy us. When we know we must control an addiction to drugs or alcohol, when we realize we must leave a destructive relationship, when we understand that we are called to confront power with truth, it may seem that we will be lost in the process. Much like Isaiah watching as the hot coal approaches his lips, it might seem that we are unable to survive the burning approach of God determined to make us new. This passage suggests that if it is God who initiates the transformation, we will survive. The angel who changes us also protects us. The fire will burn us, but it will not destroy us. As finite as we are, as sinful as we are, God's infinite grace can transform us. Through that grace, we can become new persons and find ourselves able to say with Isaiah: "Here I am . . . ; send me!"

The throne-visions of Ezekiel and Isaiah have left a deep impression on the biblical tradition. When the book of Revelation in the New Testament presents a vision of God's court to the prophet, John of Patmos, it draws upon the images that Ezekiel and Isaiah have provided. In Revelation 4:6-8, John sees God seated on a throne:

> [6]In front of the throne was something that resembled a sea of glass like crystal.
>
> In the center and around the throne, there were four living creatures covered with eyes in front and in back. [7]The first creature resembled a lion, the second was like a calf, the third had a face like that of a human being, and the fourth looked like an eagle in flight. [8]The four living creatures, each of them with six wings, were covered with eyes inside and out. Day and night they do not stop exclaiming:
> "Holy, holy, holy is the Lord God almighty,
>   who was, and who is, and who is to come."

The book of Revelation has taken the four faces of the cherubim in Ezekiel and the six wings and hymn of Isaiah and combined them to create its own vision of God's court. Within the Catholic Church, the hymn of the living creatures has become a regular part of communal worship as their triple "holy" marks the beginning of every eucharistic prayer. The four living creatures have also been associated in later tradition with the four evangelists of the Christian Gospels: the lion for Mark, the calf for Luke, the human being for Matthew, and the eagle for John.

Holy Ground

Genesis 28:10-17

Jacob's Dream at Bethel. [10]Jacob departed from Beer-sheba and proceeded toward Haran. [11]When he came upon a certain place, he stopped there for the night, since the sun had already set. Taking one of the stones at the place, he put it under his head and lay down in that place. [12]Then he had a dream: a stairway rested on the ground, with its top reaching to the heavens; and God's angels were going up and down on it. [13]And there was the LORD standing beside him and saying: I am the LORD, the God of Abraham your father and the God of Isaac; the land on which you are lying I will give to you and your descendants. [14]Your descendants will be like the dust of the earth, and through them you will spread to the west and the east, to the north and the south. In you and your descendants all the families of the earth will find blessing. [15]I am with you and will protect you wherever you go, and bring you back to this land. I will never leave you until I have done what I promised you.

[16]When Jacob awoke from his sleep, he said, "Truly, the LORD is in this place and I did not know it!" [17]He was afraid and said: "How awesome this place is! This is nothing else but the house of God, the gateway to heaven!"

As we have seen, the primary ministry of angels is to worship God in the heavenly court. Yet God's holiness is not confined to heaven. A hint of this truth is found in the song of the seraphim in Isaiah 6:3: "All the earth is filled with his glory!" The glory of God affects the world. The Bible presents numerous passages in which God's holiness and creation meet. When God speaks to Moses from the burning bush, God says, "Remove your sandals from your feet, for the place where you stand is holy ground" (Exod 3:5). An encounter with the Holy One renders the place of encounter holy. Angels are often shown to mediate God's holiness to the earth. When the angel who commands the army of the Lord appears to Joshua, he says, "Remove your sandals from your feet, for the place on which you are standing is holy" (Josh 5:15).

The most dramatic account of angels mediating God's glory is a story of the patriarch Jacob in Genesis 28:10-17 (above). This story situates Jacob in "a certain place" (v. 11). The lack of a name for the place is intentional. The point of the story is that Jacob is not aware that holiness exists in the place where he chooses to rest. He is merely making his way from Beer-sheba to Haran and stops for the night. But his dream reveals that this seemingly ordinary place is in fact a doorway to the divine. His dream reveals a stairway with angels moving up and down on it. An overnight stop becomes a gateway to heaven.

 The Hebrew word *sullam*, used in Genesis 28:12 to denote the structure on which the angels ascend and descend from heaven, only appears once in the entire Old Testament. In older translations, *sullam* is often translated as "ladder," but the term more likely refers to a stair-like structure similar to the Babylonian temples known as "ziggurats." Ziggurats were large pyramidal constructions with a series of steps leading to a summit that was believed to be the dwelling of a god.

Contemporary Relevance: The ordinary things in our lives always bear the possibility of divine encounter. A smile from a stranger, the touch of a friend, or a phone call that comes just as we need it can pull back the curtain from the mundane and reveal the Holy One. This passage asks us to see every place as that "certain place" where Jacob chooses to sleep. We can never demand or orchestrate God's presence. But we can always be prepared for God's arrival. In any circumstance we can suddenly "awake" to see not only the ordinary scene around us but a glorious highway trodden by angels, revealing the holiness of God.

This lesson has led us to unexpected places. It has discussed the cherubim and seraphim as attendants of the heavenly council. It has explored that the primary ministry of the angels is one of worship and praise. It has offered a description of angels with multiple faces and hooved feet and has even suggested that the Bible can picture angels as serpents. Most of these descriptions of the cherubim and seraphim have not carried over into the Christian imagination. We do not today see angels as sphinxes or snakes. But we should not end this lesson without noting what is surely the most widely known contribution to the way we picture angels in both the Christian tradition and popular culture: it is from the imagery of cherubim and seraphim that angels receive their wings!

The Ziggurat of Ur in modern-day Iraq.

EXPLORING LESSON TWO

1. This lesson has argued that the primary ministry of angels is to praise God. Would you say this function is more important than any other? Why or why not?

_____

_____

_____

_____

_____

_____

2. What does the word "cherubim" mean, and where does Ezekiel locate the cherubim in his vision (Ezek 1:22-27)?

_____

_____

_____

_____

_____

_____

3. In what two ways does the vision of Ezekiel associate the cherubim with creation? What value do you see in having creation represented at God's throne?

_____

_____

_____

_____

4. a) What significance might we find in the fact that Ezekiel receives his vision while in exile (Ezek 1:1-3)?

_____

_____

_____

_____

_____

b) Has God ever come to you in a time when you felt "exiled" from a person, place, or experience?

_____

_____

_____

_____

_____

5. This lesson has suggested that we may at times picture God as too much like ourselves, thus underplaying God's transcendence. Do you agree? What advantage do you see in God being "other"?

_____

_____

_____

_____

_____

_____

6. Were you surprised to find that the seraphim of Isaiah's vision might be pictured as serpents (Isa 6:1-8)? Do you feel such an image can add anything to our appreciation of angels?

_____

_____

_____

_____

_____

7. Isaiah experienced transformation by contact with a burning coal (Isa 6:7). Have you ever been afraid of a transformation or change in your life? How was God present?

_____

_____

_____

_____

_____

8. What possible meaning do the four faces of the cherubim carry in Ezekiel (1:1-28), Revelation (4:6-8), and in later Christian tradition?

_____

_____

_____

_____

_____

_____

9. Jacob recognized in his dream that he was sleeping in a holy place in the presence of angels (Gen 28:10-17). Have you ever experienced a time when an ordinary place became a divine one?

_____

_____

_____

_____

_____

_____

10. What are some of the angelic images that you recall from this lesson? Have any of these images changed the way you imagine angels? In what way?

_____

_____

_____

_____

_____

_____

CLOSING PRAYER

Prayer

Then I heard the voice of the Lord saying,
"Whom shall I send? Who will go for us?"
"Here I am," I said; "send me!"   (Isa 6:8)

Lord, may we never let a sense of our own unworthiness deter us from serving you. Open our hearts so we are aware of your call when it comes, and inspire us so we may be faithful servants in whatever work you call us to do. Today we pray especially for the strength to . . .

LESSON THREE

Speaking for God:
Angels as Messengers
of Joy and Guidance

Begin your personal study and group discussion with a simple and sincere prayer such as:

Prayer

God of heaven and earth, may our time of study and reflection lead us to imitate the angels as heralds of your word and proclaimers of your glory.

Read pages 40–51 , Lesson Three.

Respond to the questions on pages 52–54, Exploring Lesson Three.

The Closing Prayer on page 55 is for your personal use and may be used at the end of group discussion.

SPEAKING FOR GOD: ANGELS AS MESSENGERS OF JOY AND GUIDANCE

While the primary ministry of angels is worshiping God, the most common ministry of angels in the Bible is communication. Angels are routinely portrayed as messengers of God's will and purpose. The messages they deliver are most often joyous announcements of a birth or divine guidance offered to those who wish to follow God's will. In this lesson, we will explore several stories in which angels act as messengers of joy and guidance.

Joyous Births: Samson

Judges 13:2-24

The Birth of Samson. ²There was a certain man from Zorah, of the clan of the Danites, whose name was Manoah. His wife was barren and had borne no children. ³An angel of the LORD appeared to the woman and said to her: Though you are barren and have had no children, you will conceive and bear a son. ⁴Now, then, be careful to drink no wine or beer and to eat nothing unclean, ⁵for you will conceive and bear a son. No razor shall touch his head, for the boy is to be a nazirite for God from the womb. It is he who will begin to save Israel from the power of the Philistines.

⁶The woman went and told her husband, "A man of God came to me; he had the appearance of an angel of God, fearsome indeed. I did not ask him where he came from, nor did he tell me his name. ⁷But he said to me, 'You will conceive and bear a son. So drink no wine or beer, and eat nothing unclean. For the boy shall be a nazirite for God from the womb, until the day of his death.'"

⁸Manoah then prayed to the LORD. "Please, my Lord," he said, "may the man of God whom you sent return to us to teach us what to do for the boy who is to be born."

⁹God heard the prayer of Manoah, and the angel of God came again to the woman as she was sitting in the field; but her husband Manoah was not with her. ¹⁰The woman ran quickly and told her husband. "The man who came to me the other day has appeared to me," she said to him; ¹¹so Manoah got up and followed his wife. When he reached the man, he said to him, "Are you the one who spoke to my wife?" I am, he answered. ¹²Then Manoah asked, "Now, when what you say comes true, what rules must the boy follow? What must he do?" ¹³The angel of the LORD answered Manoah: Your wife must be careful about all the things of which I spoke to her. ¹⁴She must not eat anything that comes from the vine, she must not drink wine or beer, and she must not eat anything unclean. Let her observe all that I have commanded her. ¹⁵Then Manoah said to the angel of the LORD, "Permit us to detain you, so that we may prepare a young goat for you." ¹⁶But the angel of the LORD answered Manoah: Though you detained me, I would not eat your food. But if you want to prepare a burnt offering, then offer it up to the LORD. For Manoah did not know that he was the angel of the LORD. ¹⁷Then Manoah said to the angel of the LORD, "What is your name, that we may honor you when your words come true?" ¹⁸The angel of the LORD answered him:

> Why do you ask my name? It is wondrous. ¹⁹Then Manoah took a young goat with a grain offering and offered it on the rock to the LORD, who works wonders. While Manoah and his wife were looking on, ²⁰as the flame rose to the heavens from the altar, the angel of the LORD ascended in the flame of the altar. When Manoah and his wife saw this, they fell on their faces to the ground; ²¹but the angel of the LORD was seen no more by Manoah and his wife. Then Manoah, realizing that it was the angel of the LORD, ²²said to his wife, "We will certainly die, for we have seen God." ²³But his wife said to him, "If the LORD had meant to kill us, he would not have accepted a burnt offering and grain offering from our hands! Nor would he have let us see all this, or hear what we have heard."
>
> ²⁴The woman bore a son and named him Samson, and when the boy grew up the LORD blessed him.

The Bible recognizes that few events are more joyous than the birth of a child. Therefore, when God is prepared to bring a new life into the world, that gift is announced. An angel is frequently involved. In Lesson One we saw how the births of Ishmael and Isaac were communicated by a messenger angel who eventually "slipped" into God's own presence. In many other birth announcements, however, the good news is communicated by angels alone.

One such announcement concerns Samson's birth. Samson was a judge of Israel, one of a series of charismatic leaders who God raised up as Israel fought fiercely over the land of Canaan. In the book of Judges, an angel of the Lord appears to tell of Samson's birth and to instruct that he shall be raised as a "nazirite" before God. "Nazirite" comes from a Hebrew word which means "to separate, consecrate, or abstain." Nazirites separated themselves from ordinary believers by assuming a set of prescribed practices. Among these practices were abstinence from fermented beverages and refraining from cutting one's hair.

In this passage from Judges 13, an angel appears to tell of Samson's birth and to direct his life toward nazirite practices. This announcement is constructed in an elaborate and insightful manner. The angel comes not once but twice. The angel refuses to eat or share his name. But what is most interesting about this passage is the way it offers us an honest and sympathetic example of married life.

In many marriages there is a partner who leads and a partner who follows. This is true of Samson's parents, but the one who leads is surprising, considering the patriarchal culture of the ancient world. We would expect that the man would lead his family, but even though Manoah is mentioned frequently in the story, he is not the leading character. Instead, his wife is. Although her name is never given to us, she is attentive, intelligent, and deferential. It is to her that the angel appears both times (vv. 3 and 9). She senses from the first appearance that the "man of God" who speaks to her is no mortal. She tells her husband that he had "the appearance of an angel of God, fearsome indeed." Out of respect for the angel's high status, she does not question him about his origins or his name (v. 6).

Samson's father is less gifted than his wife. He is simple, uninteresting, and insensitive. When his wife informs him that they are to have a son, he does not accept her words as sufficient. Instead he prays that the angel come again and provide further instructions (v. 8). His prayer indicates his uncertainty about the angel's message that has come through his wife and implies that such a message should have included him as well.

Manoah's prayer is heard. The angel returns but again comes only to the woman (v. 9). She dutifully runs to tell her husband and leads him back to the angel. At this point Manoah "takes charge." His manner is rude and aggressive. He does not greet the angel but begins at once to question him—something that his wife had the sensitivity to avoid. Bluntly he asks, "Are you the one who spoke to [the woman]?" (v. 11). Although the English translation reads "my wife," the original Hebrew is more generic: "the woman." The omission of the more personal and respectful "my wife" further indicates the disregard Manoah has for his wife's testimony. The angel affirms that he is the one who appeared. But when Manoah presses him to give information on what rules the child should follow, the angel simply repeats what he told the woman (v. 13). It is as if the angel is saying, "We could have avoided this second visit if you had listened to your wife in the first place."

When Manoah offers to feed the angel, he refuses (vv. 15-16). When Manoah asks the angel's name, he declines to share it (vv. 17-18). Manoah still does not realize that the visitor is an angel of the Lord (v. 16). It is only when Manoah sees the angel ascend in the flames of his sacrifice that he concludes an angel has been present (v. 21). Then he fears for his life because he understands that he was in the presence of the holy. (Note that Manoah makes a direct connection between the presence of the angel and the presence of the Lord.) It is his wife who has the common sense to calm him. She argues that if the Lord meant to kill them, he would not have come to speak to them in the first place (v. 23). Throughout the entire scene, Manoah is trying to catch up with his wife. She is the one who receives the message, she is the one who first recognizes the angel, and she is the one who has the wisdom to recognize God's plan. When we read that "Manoah got up and followed his wife" (v. 11), we are not just being informed about geographical positioning. Manoah's wife is the leader of the family.

The fear Manoah expresses in Judges 13:22 that he and his wife will die because they have seen God is a common motif in the Old Testament. It was assumed that **the sight of God** would be too much for human beings to endure and would result in instant death. Even Moses, who spoke with God "face to face" (Num 12:8), was denied his request to see God in all his glory, for as God himself told Moses, "[N]o one can see me and live" (Exod 33:20).

We might note that even though the narrative presents Manoah as dull and insensitive, it does not demean him. This passage presents a sympathetic portrayal of how two unequal characters can make a marriage work. Manoah is slow to see, but he is not an overbearing patriarch. He is a man in over his head who depends on his wife and is not self-reflective enough to recognize it. Moreover, he is the only one who does not recognize this reality. God sees it. God knows that Manoah is not humble enough to receive a divine message through his wife, and so God is willing to send the angel a second time. The angel also sees it. He patiently repeats the message he already gave and politely responds to the probing questions Manoah places before him. Manoah's wife also knows her husband. She probably anticipates that he will be annoyed that the message did not come to him. She repeats the message carefully and listens quietly at Manoah's side as the angel repeats it again. She waits until her husband grasps what she already knows and then suggests the obvious to allay his fears.

Of the three characters in this story, only Manoah has a name. His wife is nameless, and the angel refuses to give his name. This detail connects the angel and the woman. Manoah has a name but no insight. The angel and the woman are united in knowing God's plan and are indulgent of the man who struggles to catch up.

Contemporary Relevance: We are not all the same. Some of us have an affinity for the spiritual. Others struggle to believe. Some avoid attention and notoriety, wishing only to love and be loved. Others are wedded to names and titles to which they attach their value and status. The story of Samson's birth suggests that love and acceptance are possible across such differences. The story presents a nameless woman and angel who patiently and lovingly bear with Manoah. He is limited and slow to recognize God's action. But the woman and the angel who understand the holy respect Manoah enough to overlook his blind spots and work with his imperfections.

Through the characters it presents to us—human, angelic, and divine—this story invites us to show kindness to those whose gifts are less than ours. It reminds us that the greatest grace is not our individual aptitudes and abilities but the manner in which we use them to build common ground with one another. When we reach across our differences in a friendship, work relationship, or marriage, we allow love to flourish between unequal partners. The angel who arrives to announce new life, then, is also the bearer of patience and consideration. It is only with these qualities of love and acceptance that all may rejoice together in the new life God is about to give.

Joyous Births: John the Baptist and Jesus
Luke 1:5-38

Announcement of the Birth of John. ⁵In the days of Herod, King of Judea, there was a priest named Zechariah of the priestly division of Abijah; his wife was from the daughters of Aaron, and her name was Elizabeth. ⁶Both were righteous in the eyes of God, observing all the commandments and ordinances of the Lord blamelessly. ⁷But they had no child, because Elizabeth was barren and both were advanced in years. ⁸Once when he was serving as priest in his division's turn before God, ⁹according to the practice of the priestly service, he was chosen by lot to enter the sanctuary of the Lord to burn incense. ¹⁰Then, when the whole assembly of the people was praying outside at the hour of the incense offering, ¹¹the angel of the Lord appeared to him, standing at the right of the altar of incense. ¹²Zechariah was troubled by what he saw, and fear came upon him. ¹³But the angel said to him, "Do not be afraid, Zechariah, because your prayer has been heard. Your wife Elizabeth will bear you a son, and you shall name him John. ¹⁴And you will have joy and gladness, and many will rejoice at his birth, ¹⁵for he will be great in the sight of [the] Lord. He will drink neither wine nor strong drink. He will be

filled with the holy Spirit even from his mother's womb, ¹⁶and he will turn many of the children of Israel to the Lord their God. ¹⁷He will go before him in the spirit and power of Elijah to turn the hearts of fathers toward children and the disobedient to the understanding of the righteous, to prepare a people fit for the Lord." ¹⁸Then Zechariah said to the angel, "How shall I know this? For I am an old man, and my wife is advanced in years." ¹⁹And the angel said to him in reply, "I am Gabriel, who stand before God. I was sent to speak to you and to announce to you this good news. ²⁰But now you will be speechless and unable to talk until the day these things take place, because you did not believe my words, which will be fulfilled at their proper time."

²¹Meanwhile the people were waiting for Zechariah and were amazed that he stayed so long in the sanctuary. ²²But when he came out, he was unable to speak to them, and they realized that he had seen a vision in the sanctuary. He was gesturing to them but remained mute. ²³Then, when his days of ministry were completed, he went home. ²⁴After this time his wife Elizabeth conceived, and she went into seclusion for five months, saying, ²⁵"So has the Lord done for me at a time when he has seen fit to take away my disgrace before others."

Announcement of the Birth of Jesus. ²⁶In the sixth month, the angel Gabriel was sent from God to a town of Galilee called Nazareth, ²⁷to a virgin betrothed to a man named Joseph, of the house of David, and the virgin's name was Mary. ²⁸And coming to her, he said, "Hail, favored one! The Lord is with you." ²⁹But she was greatly troubled at what was said and pondered what sort of greeting this might be. ³⁰Then the angel said to her, "Do not be afraid, Mary, for you have found favor with God. ³¹Behold, you will conceive in your womb and bear a son, and you shall name him Jesus. ³²He will be great and will be called Son of the Most High, and the Lord God will give him the throne of David his father, ³³and he will rule over the house of Jacob forever, and of his kingdom there will be no end." ³⁴But Mary said to the

continue

angel, "How can this be, since I have no relations with a man?" 35And the angel said to her in reply, "The holy Spirit will come upon you, and the power of the Most High will overshadow you. Therefore the child to be born will be called holy, the Son of God. 36And behold, Elizabeth, your relative, has also conceived a son in her old age, and this is the sixth month for her who was called barren; 37for nothing will be impossible for God." 38Mary said, "Behold, I am the handmaid of the Lord. May it be done to me according to your word." Then the angel departed from her.

The Gospel of Luke begins with two birth announcements, that of John the Baptist and that of Jesus. Luke has carefully constructed these back-to-back accounts to mirror each other, so considering them together is helpful.

In these two accounts, an angel announces a birth first to a father and then to a mother. The announcement of John's birth is made to his father Zechariah, while that of Jesus' birth is made to his mother Mary. Both announcements follow each other step by step. The parents are introduced and are without children (vv. 5-7 and 26-27). The angel Gabriel appears (vv. 11 and 28). Both Zechariah and Mary are troubled (vv. 12 and 29). Gabriel tells both not to fear (vv. 13 and 30). The births are announced along with the name of each child (vv. 13 and 31). Something of the life of each child is revealed (vv. 14-17 and 32-33). Both Zechariah and Mary question what the angel is telling them (vv. 18 and 34). Gabriel reasserts the message with assurance (vv. 19 and 35). A sign confirming the announcement is given by the angel (vv. 20 and 36-37).

These two birth announcements mirror each other and show the closeness between John the Baptist and Jesus. The announcement of John's birth was important enough to share the same structure as the announcement of Jesus' birth. This high regard for John is expressed later in the Gospel when Jesus says, "I tell you, among those born of women, no one is greater than John" (Luke 7:28). Nevertheless, even as Luke demonstrates John's high position, he also emphasizes the superiority of Jesus. The parallelism of the two announcements is a "step parallelism": Jesus is always a step above John. John's birth is wondrous because of the ad-

 Biblical birth announcements tend to share a similar pattern as seen in the chart below.

	Isaac Genesis 18	Samson Judges 13	John the Baptist Luke 1:5-25	Jesus Luke 1:26-38
Appearance of the Lord (or angel)	18:1-2	13:3, 10	1:10-11	1:26
Sign of fear or reverence	18:2		1:12	1:29
Divine promise: **a son will be born;** **this is his name;** **this is his future**	18:10	13:3 13:5	1:13 1:13 1:15-17	1:31a 1:31b 1:32-33
Objection	18:12	13:8	1:18	1:34
Reassurance/sign	18:13-14	13:19-20	1:19	1:35-36

vanced age of his parents, while Jesus' birth is wondrous because it happens without a human father. John will be great in the sight of the Lord, but Jesus will be the Son of the Most High. Zechariah doubts the angel's message, but Mary accepts it. The sign for Zechariah is the loss of speech, while the sign for Mary is new life in her cousin, Elizabeth.

Luke ties the joy and wonder of these announcements to the story of Abraham and Sarah in Genesis 18:1-15. Gabriel's words "nothing will be impossible for God" (v. 37) are an echo of God's words to Abraham: "Is anything too marvelous for the LORD to do?" (Gen 18:14). Luke is also aware of Sarah's laughter indicating her doubtful reaction to the announcement of her pregnancy. Both Zechariah

and Mary question the angel. Zechariah's doubt prevents him from believing, while Mary asks for clarification and then accepts the angel's message. Yet even Mary does not receive the announcement without an initial reservation.

Contemporary Relevance: These birth announcements remind us that when God promises something truly wonderful, we are not required to believe immediately. We often struggle to accept God's wondrous invitations. But our effort to accept God's good news should not be judged harshly. In fact, the questions that arise in our hearts are an indication that we know God is real and has the power to bless us. If even the mother of God questions the angel, we are all free to raise our concerns before God's messengers.

 Angels Rejoice at the Birth of Jesus

Although angels often serve as God's messengers at the announcement of a birth, there is only one time in the Bible when angels rejoice at a birth itself:

> [8]Now there were shepherds in that region living in the fields and keeping the night watch over their flock. [9]The angel of the Lord appeared to them and the glory of the Lord shone around them, and they were struck with great fear. [10]The angel said to them, "Do not be afraid; for behold, I proclaim to you good news of great joy that will be for all the people. [11]For today in the city of David a savior has been born for you who is Messiah and Lord. [12]And this will be a sign for you: you will find an infant wrapped in swaddling clothes and lying in a manger." [13]And suddenly there was a multitude of the heavenly host with the angel, praising God and saying:
>
> [14] "Glory to God in the highest
>   and on earth peace to those on whom his favor rests" (Luke 2:8-14).

There are two parts to this passage: an announcement (vv. 8-12) and a heavenly revelation (vv. 13-14). The announcement of the angel to the shepherds follows the pattern of the birth announcements of John and Jesus (see page 44). The shepherds are introduced (v. 8). The "angel of the Lord" (likely Gabriel; see 1:11, 19, 26) appears, and the shepherds are overcome with fear (v. 9). The angel tells them not to fear, proclaims that Jesus' birth has taken place, and reveals something of his identity (vv. 10-11). A sign is given by the angel (v. 12). All that is lacking in this pattern is questioning or objection by the shepherds. This is most likely because there can be little doubt about a birth that has already taken place.

The announcement of the angel is followed by a heavenly revelation. The sky opens, and the shepherds hear praise of God coming from the angelic hosts (v. 14). Clearly the shepherds have been privileged with a view into the throne room of God.

The rabbis taught that when God finished the work of creation, the angels sang a hymn of praise. They do the same here because the great saving work of God has begun with Jesus' birth.

Divine Guidance: Abraham

Genesis 22:1-19

Angels not only communicate the joyful news of a birth. They also give guidance to follow God's will. Sometimes this direction is to cease and desist. This is the case in what may be the most distressing passage in the Bible: Genesis 22:1-19 (I will paraphrase the story here, but you may wish to look it up in your Bible and read it in full).

At the beginning of the story, without any warning, God says to Abraham, "Take your son Isaac, your only one, whom you love, and go to the land of Moriah. There offer him up as a burnt offering on one of the heights that I will point out to you" (v. 2).

God's command stops our breath. It is monstrous and irrational. Isaac was a longed-for and long-awaited son. His birth occurred when Abraham and Sarah were advanced in age. Isaac is the fulfillment of God's promise to Abraham and the hope for the future of God's people. But now God demands that Abraham kill Isaac. To be sure, verse 1 tells us that God is testing Abraham ("God put Abraham to the test"). But what a horrific test! What kind of God would ask a father to do such a thing?

Abraham obeys God's command. He takes his son Isaac and journeys to Moriah. He builds an altar, arranges the wood upon it, binds Isaac to the wood, and takes out a knife to slaughter his son. The story is told with deliberate detachment. One detail builds upon the next towards the fearful climax. It is with relief, then, that an angel appears: "But the angel of the LORD called to him from heaven, 'Abraham, Abraham!' 'Here I am,' he answered. 'Do not lay your hand on the boy,' said the angel. 'Do not do the least thing to him. For now I know that you fear God, since you did not withhold from me your son, your only one'" (vv. 11-12). The angel averts the slaughter, and Isaac is spared. But we are left aghast at God's horrifying test.

Two points are helpful for understanding this difficult passage. First, we should realize that behind this ancient text lies the practice of human sacrifice. Some primitive religions believed that the sacrifice of what was most dear, a son or daughter, would be pleasing to their gods. This barbaric practice is even found in the history of Israel. Kings Ahaz and Manasseh immolated their children by fire (2 Kgs 3:27, 21:6). Therefore, with all its difficulties, it is to the credit of this narrative that it insists human sacrifice will not be accepted by the God of Israel.

Secondly, however we read this story, we must not read it as a literal description of God. God does not toy with parents, threatening their children to test their faith. One rabbinic interpretation of this passage insists that Abraham certainly misunderstood God, for God would never ask for the death of a child. Following that suggestion, this story is best understood as Abraham's misguided belief that God would find the sacrifice of Isaac acceptable. The appearance of the angel, then, becomes the moment when Abraham's misunderstanding is revealed by a messenger from God.

Contemporary Relevance: This passage is worth remembering in a world where individuals, factions, and political movements claim that religious motivation can make violent and unjust actions acceptable in God's sight. Those who seek power and control can easily call upon God's support for their partisan and political agendas. Once God's name is engaged on their behalf, it may seem that any means can be justified. This story of Abraham insists that God is not pleased with wars and coercion, even if God's name is enlisted to support them. When we encounter such warped religious thought, the words of the angel are directed to us: "Do not lay your hand on the boy. Do not do the least thing to him."

Divine Guidance: Balaam

Numbers 22:22-35

The book of Numbers recounts Israel's journey to the Promised Land. Neighboring kingdoms are threatened by Israel's approach. Balak, King of Moab, worries that this new group will exhaust the resources of the land

and in time challenge his authority. To stop Israel's progress, Balak approaches a famous seer of the region and asks him to curse Israel. The seer's name is Balaam, and he agrees to Balak's request and begins to journey to Moab. God, however, is not pleased with Balaam's decision and uses an angel to communicate divine dissatisfaction in Numbers 22:22-35. But what sets this story apart and makes it so memorable is that God uses a donkey!

The Talking Donkey. ²²But now God's anger flared up at him [Balaam] for going, and the angel of the LORD took up a position on the road as his adversary. As Balaam was riding along on his donkey, accompanied by two of his servants, ²³the donkey saw the angel of the LORD standing in the road with sword drawn. The donkey turned off the road and went into the field, and Balaam beat the donkey to bring her back on the road. ²⁴Then the angel of the LORD stood in a narrow lane between vineyards with a stone wall on each side. ²⁵When the donkey saw the angel of the LORD there, she pressed against the wall; and since she squeezed Balaam's leg against the wall, he beat her again. ²⁶Then the angel of the LORD again went ahead, and stood next in a passage so narrow that there was no room to move either to the right or to the left. ²⁷When the donkey saw the angel of the LORD there, she lay down under Balaam. Balaam's anger flared up and he beat the donkey with his stick.

²⁸Then the LORD opened the mouth of the donkey, and she asked Balaam, "What have I done to you that you beat me these three times?" ²⁹"You have acted so willfully against me," said Balaam to the donkey, "that if I only had a sword at hand, I would kill you here and now." ³⁰But the donkey said to Balaam, "Am I not your donkey, on which you have always ridden until now? Have I been in the habit of treating you this way before?" "No," he replied.

³¹Then the LORD opened Balaam's eyes, so that he saw the angel of the LORD standing on the road with sword drawn; and he knelt and bowed down to the ground. ³²But the angel of the LORD said to him: "Why have you beaten your donkey these three times? I have come as an adversary because this rash journey of yours is against my will. ³³When the donkey saw me, she turned away from me these three times. If she had not turned away from me, you are the one I would have killed, though I would have spared her." ³⁴Then Balaam said to the angel of the LORD, "I have sinned. Yet I did not know that you took up a position to oppose my journey. Since it has displeased you, I will go back home." ³⁵But the angel of the LORD said to Balaam: "Go with the men; but you may say only what I tell you." So Balaam went on with the princes of Balak.

The roots of this story are found in the early folklore of Israel. The passage both entertains and educates. The irony of the story is deep. Balaam is a professional "seer" whom the rulers of the region approach for insight, yet he cannot see the angel of the Lord standing on the road before him with a drawn sword (v. 23). But the donkey can! Three times she tries to protect her master from the fearsome angel. Readers can sympathize with the frantic beast as she attempts to squeeze past the angel who stands in a narrow-walled lane (v. 25). She is

Balaam and his donkey encounter an angel. Engraving by Julius Schnorr von Carolsfeld (1794–1872).

doing her best, but all she receives are beatings for her efforts. Because Balaam does not see the angel, he interprets the actions of his animal as obstinacy. Even when the donkey begins to speak to him, Balaam is so focused on what he perceives to be true that he does not sense he is missing something. Only when the Lord opens his eyes to see the angel does he realize his blindness (v. 31).

Contemporary Relevance: This story reminds us that God can use any person or thing to speak to us and that humble and unexpected creatures are often God's preference. God is not limited to lofty and beautiful messengers. Moreover, our talents and expertise can themselves limit our vision. Balaam was a professional "seer," yet he could not see. We should always be grateful for our gifts and abilities. But we should also remember that the confidence we place in them can distract us when God chooses to bypass them. God often works through us, but God can also work without us. This is why we should listen for God's voice—not only in the places we know well but also in the places we would never expect. As wise as we may be, God can still speak to us through the lowly.

Paul understood this mystery: "God chose the foolish of the world to shame the wise, and God chose the weak of the world to shame the strong, and God chose the lowly and despised of the world, those who count for nothing, to reduce to nothing those who are something, so that no human being might boast before God" (1 Cor 1:27-29). When God wishes to speak to us, angels are available. But sometimes even donkeys have words to say.

Divine Guidance: The Book of Acts

Acts 8:26-40; 10:1–11:18

Throughout the book of Acts, the Spirit of God guides the early church as the good news about Jesus spreads from Jerusalem to the ends of the earth. Step by step the Spirit leads the apostles to accomplish God's will. Even though God communicates most frequently through the Spirit in the book of Acts, there are times when God sends angels. This happens to the apostle Philip (Acts 8:26-40). While proclaiming the gospel in Samaria, Philip receives divine direction: "Then the angel of the Lord spoke to Philip, 'Get up and head south on the road that goes down from Jerusalem to Gaza, the desert route'" (8:26). Philip follows the angel's direction and meets an Ethiopian eunuch. He preaches the gospel to him and baptizes him.

 At first glance, **Philip** appears to be the protagonist in Acts 8:26-40, the one who keeps the story moving. In fact, however, it is the angel of the Lord (8:26) or the Spirit of the Lord (8:29, 39) who propels Philip forward. Philip effectively models for us what can happen when we are open to God acting through us.

Philip was given an opportunity when he heard the Ethiopian reading aloud and recognized the words of the prophet Isaiah. Already open to the action of God in him, Philip ran to the chariot to open the words of the prophet and to "proclaim Jesus."

This story of Philip reminds us that when we are responsive to God's life in us, we too will find opportunities to witness to others about Jesus—sometimes with our words, and more often with our actions and attitudes.

A more complex and important communication by an angel in the book of Acts, however, takes place in chapters 10 and 11. This is a major turning point in Acts and in the early church. In these chapters the apostles begin to realize that the gospel of Jesus Christ is not only for Jews but also Gentiles. To accentuate this dramatic realization, Luke, the author of Acts, has constructed a complex narrative involving the gentile Cornelius and the apostle Peter: an angel appears to Cornelius, and a vision is given to Peter. The intersection of these two events becomes the means for God's will to become known.

The story begins in the city of Caesarea. Cornelius, a Gentile, sees an angel who tells him to send for the apostle Peter who is in Joppa. Cornelius understands that this is God's will and sends some men to find Peter (10:1-8). Meanwhile, Peter is given a vision in Joppa (10:9-16). A large sheet comes down from heaven holding all the animals on earth. A voice says to Peter, "Slaughter and eat" (10:13). Since Jews were permitted to eat only certain animals, Peter objects. The vision occurs three times, but Peter does not understand what it means. While he is trying to make sense of it, the men arrive inviting him to Cornelius's house. The Spirit tells Peter to go with them, and he does (10:17-23). Peter does not yet understand the vision, but its connection to the invitation from Cornelius leads him to believe that God is at work.

When Peter arrives at Caesarea, Cornelius welcomes him. Although Peter should not visit a Gentile's home, he begins to see that his vision and this visit are connected. Cornelius tells him how the angel directed him to invite Peter to his house (10:24-33). Subsequently when Peter preaches (10:34-43), the Holy Spirit descends on all present and Cornelius and his family are baptized (10:44-48). Peter now sees that God invites all, Jews and Gentiles, to faith in Jesus. After a few days, Jewish believers call Peter to Jerusalem to explain why he is visiting and baptizing Gentiles (11:1-18). Peter again recounts his vision and the angel's visit to Cornelius. He tells how he preached and the Holy Spirit descended. He concludes, "If then God gave them the same gift he gave to us when we came to believe in the Lord Jesus Christ, who was I to be able to hinder God?" (11:17). Now the entire church understands that God's will is to welcome Gentiles into the church.

Contemporary Relevance: The angelic announcement to Cornelius and the vision of Peter come together to reveal God's will for the early church—a revelation that changed the course of the church and indeed the course of human history. The complex way in which Luke tells this story reminds us that God can work on several fronts at once. Using an angel in Caesarea and a vision in Joppa, God coordinates several streams of grace to bring about the divine purpose: the salvation of the entire world.

When we, like Peter, are confronted with a message that seems confusing and contrary, our responsibility is to discover its meaning. Yet even as we strive to understand what is unfolding, we can also trust that God is already working through other events to make the message clear. God is coming to us from several directions. Perhaps an issue at work is clarified by an unrelated comment by one of our children, or a problem with a friend is understood through a podcast we find online. God's plan is much bigger and more complex than our own. Therefore, when we realize that we do not have all that we need to resolve an issue or problem in our lives, the sensible approach is to wait and watch for the next piece of the puzzle that God will surely put into place.

The Greatest Message of Joy: The Paschal Mystery

Of all the joyful news announced in the Bible, none is more important for Christians than the paschal mystery. Jesus' death, resurrection, and future return in glory form the core of the Christian faith. We might expect that this ultimate good news would be delivered by angels, and we are not disappointed.

Women discover the empty tomb on Easter morning. The Gospel of Matthew tells us that an angel from heaven came down and rolled back the stone from the tomb. The angel tells the women, "Do not be afraid! I know that you are seeking Jesus the crucified. He is not here, for he has been raised just as he said. Come and see the place where he lay" (Matt 28:5-6).

In the Gospel of Luke "two men in dazzling garments" appear to the women (Luke 24:4). Aware of the diverse ways God's messengers appear in the Bible, we recognize these two men as angels. If any confirmation of this is

Gospel Accounts of the Good News of Jesus' Resurrection

A comparison between the various Gospel accounts of the empty tomb and the announcement of the resurrection reveals several striking similarities. All four Gospels, for example, include a description of an encounter with angels (Matt 28:2-3; Mark 16:5; Luke 24:4; John 20:11-12).

Matthew 28:1-7	Mark 16:1-7	Luke 24:1-7	John 20:1, 11-17
[1]After the sabbath, as the first day of the week was dawning, Mary Magdalene and the other Mary came to see the tomb. [2]And behold, there was a great earthquake; for an angel of the Lord descended from heaven, approached, rolled back the stone, and sat upon it. [3]His appearance was like lightning and his clothing was white as snow. [4]The guards were shaken with fear of him and became like dead men. [5]Then the angel said to the women in reply, "Do not be afraid! I know that you are seeking Jesus the crucified. [6]He is not here, for he has been raised just as he said. Come and see the place where he lay. [7]Then go quickly and tell his disciples, 'He has been raised from the dead, and he is going before you to Galilee; there you will see him.' Behold, I have told you."	[1]When the sabbath was over, Mary Magdalene, Mary, the mother of James, and Salome bought spices so that they might go and anoint him. [2]Very early when the sun had risen, on the first day of the week, they came to the tomb. [3]They were saying to one another, "Who will roll back the stone for us from the entrance to the tomb?" [4]When they looked up, they saw that the stone had been rolled back; it was very large. [5]On entering the tomb they saw a young man sitting on the right side, clothed in a white robe, and they were utterly amazed. [6]He said to them, "Do not be amazed! You seek Jesus of Nazareth, the crucified. He has been raised; he is not here. Behold, the place where they laid him. [7]But go and tell his disciples and Peter, 'He is going before you to Galilee; there you will see him, as he told you.'"	[1]But at daybreak on the first day of the week they took the spices they had prepared and went to the tomb. [2]They found the stone rolled away from the tomb; [3]but when they entered, they did not find the body of the Lord Jesus. [4]While they were puzzling over this, behold, two men in dazzling garments appeared to them. [5]They were terrified and bowed their faces to the ground. They said to them, "Why do you seek the living one among the dead? [6]He is not here, but he has been raised. Remember what he said to you while he was still in Galilee, [7]that the Son of Man must be handed over to sinners and be crucified, and rise on the third day."	[1]On the first day of the week, Mary of Magdala came to the tomb early in the morning, while it was still dark, and saw the stone removed from the tomb. . . . [11]But Mary stayed outside the tomb weeping. And as she wept, she bent over into the tomb [12]and saw two angels in white sitting there, one at the head and one at the feet where the body of Jesus had been. [13]And they said to her, "Woman, why are you weeping?" She said to them, "They have taken my Lord, and I don't know where they laid him." [14]When she had said this, she turned around and saw Jesus there, but did not know it was Jesus. [15]Jesus said to her, "Woman, why are you weeping? Whom are you looking for?" She thought it was the gardener and said to him, "Sir, if you carried him away, tell me where you laid him, and I will take him." [16]Jesus said to her, "Mary!" She turned and said to him in Hebrew, "Rabbouni," which means Teacher. [17]Jesus said to her, "Stop holding on to me, for I have not yet ascended to the Father. But go to my brothers and tell them, 'I am going to my Father and your Father, to my God and your God.'"

required, we can find it in the words of the two disciples on the way to Emmaus. As they recount to Jesus the events of Easter morning, they say that some women of their group went to the tomb and did not find his body but "came back and reported that they had indeed seen a vision of angels who announced that he was alive" (Luke 24:23). Like the angel in Matthew, the two men of Luke announce the resurrection of the one who was crucified: "Why do you seek the living one among the dead? He is not here, but he has been raised. Remember what he said to you while he was still in Galilee, that the Son of Man must be handed over to sinners and be crucified, and rise on the third day" (Luke 24:5-7).

Luke's "two men" reappear at Jesus' ascension. Dressed in white garments, they stand next to the disciples as they watch Jesus being lifted up. These two angels have their own message of joy: "Men of Galilee, why are you standing there looking at the sky? This Jesus who has been taken up from you into heaven will return in the same way as you have seen him going into heaven" (Acts 1:11).

In the Gospel of Mark, the women enter the tomb to find "a young man sitting on the right side, clothed in a white robe" (Mark 16:5). Again we recognize him as an angel. He too proclaims Jesus' resurrection: "Do not be amazed! You seek Jesus of Nazareth, the crucified. He has been raised; he is not here. Behold, the place where they laid him" (Mark 16:6).

In John's Gospel, Mary Magdalene comes to the tomb alone. Weeping, she bends over into the tomb and sees "two angels in white sitting there, one at the head and one at the feet where the body of Jesus had been" (John 20:12).

The angels ask her why she is weeping, and she says that she cannot find the body of Jesus. We expect that the angels would then announce the resurrection. But before they can do so, Mary turns and sees the risen Jesus himself. He tells her he has not yet ascended to the Father but that she should "go to my brothers and tell them, 'I am going to my Father and your Father, to my God and your God'" (John 20:17). Similar to the biblical scenes where the presence of an angel suddenly "slips" into the presence of God, the angels of John's resurrection scene give way to Jesus who himself proclaims the resurrection.

Contemporary Relevance: Angels surround the great act of our salvation. They gather at the empty tomb and at the ascension to proclaim the paschal mystery. The prominence of angels at these key events of our salvation remind us of the supreme importance of Jesus' death, resurrection, and return in glory. They also capture the truth that the paschal mystery is not yet completed. Jesus' death and resurrection are behind us, but his glorious return still lies ahead. Only then will God's kingdom be fully established. What has already happened grounds our faith: Jesus is risen, and the establishment of God's kingdom has begun. Yet until Jesus returns, the plan of God is not complete. Forces against God's will continue in our world. So we wait for the day when Christ will destroy every evil and fully establish a new creation. With the angels, we stand in the midst of the paschal mystery. We look back believing that Christ is truly risen. We look forward in hope that his victory will extend to all that is. Christ has died. Christ is risen. Christ will come again!

EXPLORING LESSON THREE

1. A significant number of biblical passages in which angels speak for God are birth announcements. Why do you think a birth was so important for the biblical authors?

_____

_____

_____

_____

_____

2. a) How does the account of Manoah and his wife in Judges 13 reflect realities about marriage and relationships?

_____

_____

_____

_____

_____

   b) What is your reaction to this story and the commentary's approach to it?

_____

_____

_____

_____

_____

3. Why did Luke compose the birth announcements of John the Baptist and Jesus in a way that emphasizes the parallels between the two accounts (Luke 1:5-38)?

_____

_____

_____

_____

_____

4. Why do you think Luke included the questions of both Zechariah and Mary in these birth announcements (Luke 1:18, 34)?

_____

_____

_____

_____

_____

_____

5. Briefly describe the three scenes in which angels appear at the beginning of Luke's Gospel (Luke 1:5-23, 26-38; 2:8-14). Which one is most meaningful for you?

_____

_____

_____

_____

_____

_____

6. a) What are two ways we might understand the difficult scene in which God asks Abraham to kill his son, according to the commentary (Gen 22)?

_____

_____

_____

_____

_____

b) Do you find these interpretations helpful? What are your thoughts about this story?

_____

_____

_____

_____

_____

7. The story of Balaam reminds us that God can guide us through any person or thing, and that God often chooses to communicate through people and events that are unexpected or seemingly insignificant. Have you ever received such a message from God? How did it come to you?

_____

_____

_____

_____

_____

_____

8. The story of Cornelius and Peter in Acts purposely shows God acting on two fronts at once in order to communicate with the early church (Acts 10–11). Can you think of another example from Scripture or from your own experiences when God has spoken from several directions at once?

_____

_____

_____

_____

_____

_____

9. In all four Gospels, angels proclaim the paschal mystery (Matt 28:2-3; Mark 16:5; Luke 24:4; John 20:11-12). What are the various ways angels are presented in these accounts?

_____

_____

_____

_____

_____

_____

CLOSING PRAYER

Prayer

Then the LORD opened Balaam's eyes, so that he saw the angel of the LORD standing on the road with sword drawn; and he knelt and bowed down to the ground. (Num 22:31)

Lord, despite our best efforts we are often blinded by our pride and deafened by the sounds of the world. Help us to see the signs you send to guide us in our lives. Teach us to listen attentively to the voices that speak your words of counsel. Today we especially ask for the grace to . . .

LESSON FOUR

Ruling the Cosmos: Angels as Controlling Spirits of the Elements and Nations

Begin your personal study and group discussion with a simple and sincere prayer such as:

Prayer

God of heaven and earth, may our time of study and reflection lead us to imitate the angels as heralds of your word and proclaimers of your glory.

Read pages 58–68 , Lesson Four.

Respond to the questions on pages 69–71, Exploring Lesson Four.

The Closing Prayer on page 71 is for your personal use and may be used at the end of group discussion.

RULING THE COSMOS: ANGELS AS CONTROLLING SPIRITS OF THE ELEMENTS AND NATIONS

In Lessons Two and Three, we examined the ministries of angels as worshipers at God's throne and messengers from God to us. These roles fit easily into our typical expectation of what angels do. In this lesson we will explore a ministry that most modern believers are not aware of: the Bible presents angels as the "controlling spirits" of the world. In this ministry angels empower and guide the operation of the cosmos and the history and development of the nations.

Such a conviction is understandably foreign to modern thought. Today most of us believe that the world functions according to impersonal "laws of nature" and that nations are guided by the agreed traditions and customs of power. The biblical authors saw the world differently. To them "Egypt" and "Greece" were human collectives whose fortunes were connected to angelic beings. "Water" and "fire" were not independent elements but realities animated by specific angels. It is the challenge of this lesson to appreciate this perspective so that we can understand the biblical truths that depend upon it. We will also discuss the temptation to worship angels and the efforts within the New Testament to assert Jesus' superiority over angelic forces.

Belief in the "controlling spirits" of the world seems to have originated in a concept we have already explored: God's divine council. In Lesson Two we discussed how God's heavenly court was modeled on the courts of earthly kings and populated with an array of subservient ministers. The idea of the court was influenced by the religions of Mesopotamia and Ugarit that heavily shaped the ancient Near Eastern culture in which Israel developed as a nation. In those religions there were heavenly councils composed of the gods and goddesses of the land. Along with these major gods, there were lesser deities with whom the higher gods consulted and through whom they acted. For instance, in Mesopotamia, the high god Anu presided over the council. In Ugarit, El was the supreme god. The portrayal of Israel's God was influenced by the way the gods of these cultures were understood.

At the beginning of its history, Israel worshiped the Lord as one of many gods. This polytheistic context is clearly demonstrated in biblical passages such as the famous covenant ceremony at Shechem. In that ceremony Joshua declares, "If it is displeasing to you to serve the LORD, choose today whom you will serve, the gods your ancestors served beyond the River or the gods of the Amorites in whose country you are dwelling. As for me and my household, we will serve the LORD" (Josh 24:15). To Joshua, serving the God of Israel was one choice among a number of options.

As Israel came to believe that there was only one God, the other gods of its culture were transformed into lesser ministers of God's court. Those beings once recognized as gods in their own right became subservient to the God of Israel. In time these "lesser gods" came to be seen as angels, creatures of the one God. As angels, they retained real power, but their power was now delegated to them by the one supreme God.

An important passage in Deuteronomy illustrates this delegation:

⁸When the Most High allotted each nation its
    heritage,
    when he separated out human beings,
He set up the boundaries of the peoples
    after the number of the divine beings;
⁹But the Lᴏʀᴅ's portion was his people;
    his allotted share was Jacob. (Deut 32:8-9)

Here the God of Israel assigns a "divine being" (literally a "son of God") to each of the nations. Although all the other nations had their own controlling angels, God did not assign an angelic minister to guide Israel but kept Israel as God's own portion.

This idea of a ruling angel continued to develop over time. In the book of Daniel, an angel appears to the prophet and says, "Do you know . . . why I have come to you? Soon I must fight the prince of Persia again. When I leave, the prince of Greece will come; but I shall tell you what is written in the book of truth. No one supports me against these except Michael, your prince" (Dan 10:20-21). The "princes" of Persia and Greece of whom the angel speaks are not the historical rulers, Darius III and Alexander the Great. They are the angelic guardians of those two nations. Fighting those countries means fighting those angels. By this time, the "prince" known as Michael is considered to be the angelic prince of Israel.

It may seem strange that the God of Israel would appoint angelic ministers to pagan nations. Yet the belief in such national angels is an emerging proclamation of the universal reign of God. It insists that even the Gentile nations do not lie outside the scope of God's power. The power of foreign nations derives from the authority of the God of Israel. Whatever control Gentile nations may exercise over Israel, their authority is only possible because it was granted them by the one true God.

After the return from exile in Babylon (sixth century ʙᴄᴇ), Israel lived under the domination of one world empire after another. These overlords were often tyrannical and immoral, and their evil conduct was ascribed to the negligence or perversion of their angelic rulers.

Psalm 82 presents a dramatic scene in which God in the divine council accuses his heavenly entourage of failing to direct the nations in ways that are right. The nations over which they rule practice injustice and fail to care for the lowly and the poor. Despite their semi-divine status, God threatens them with death because of their disregard for justice:

Psalm 82:1-8

¹God takes a stand in the divine council,
    gives judgment in the midst of the gods.
²"How long will you judge unjustly
    and favor the cause of the wicked?

³"Defend the lowly and fatherless;
    render justice to the afflicted and needy.
⁴Rescue the lowly and poor;
    deliver them from the hand of the wicked."

⁵The gods neither know nor understand,
    wandering about in darkness,
    and all the world's foundations shake.
⁶I declare: "Gods though you be,
    offspring of the Most High all of you,
⁷Yet like any mortal you shall die;
    like any prince you shall fall."
⁸Arise, O God, judge the earth,
    for yours are all the nations.

The angels of God's court guide the nations, but their power comes from the one true God. In light of their failure to direct things aright, God seems willing to remove their authority.

A similar instance of angelic control is found in the book of Revelation, which presents angels as the rulers of churches. The author of Revelation, John of Patmos, was an itinerant prophet who routinely visited seven cities in Asia Minor: Ephesus, Smyrna, Pergamum, Thyatira, Sardis, Philadelphia, and Laodicea. In John's first vision he sees "one like a son of man" standing in the midst of seven lampstands and holding seven stars in his right hand (Rev 1:9-19). The vision is explained in

Revelation 1:20: "This is the secret meaning of the seven stars you saw in my right hand, and of the seven gold lampstands: the seven stars are the angels of the seven churches, and the seven lampstands are the seven churches."

The messages that Christ wishes to send to these churches take the form of letters in Revelation 2–3. The addressee of each letter is not the church community but its ruling angel. For example, the letter to the church of Ephesus begins, "To the angel of the church in Ephesus, write this" (Rev 2:1). The same format is used for the other six letters. The angels addressed should not be interpreted as guardian angels who are always in conformity with God's will. The churches' ruling angels, along with their churches, can be accused of failing to obey God's commands. The church in Sardis, for example, is told that although it boasts of a good reputation, it is in fact "dead" (Rev 3:1). The angels addressed in Revelation 2–3 are controlling angels that bear great responsibility. They are identified with their churches and rise and fall with them.

Not only are angels seen to control the fate of nations and churches, but many biblical texts present them as directing the course of the natural world. Heavenly bodies, earth's elements, and the forces of nature are understood to be ruled by particular angels. Psalm 104:4 addresses God: "You make the winds your messengers; / flaming fire, your ministers." The letter to the Hebrews later interprets this psalm in reference to angels: "Of the angels he says: / 'He makes his angels winds / and his ministers a fiery flame'" (Heb 1:7).

Angels that control the elements are also present in the book of Revelation. One angel controls the waters: "Then I heard the angel in charge of the waters say: / 'You are just, O Holy One, / who are and who were, / in passing this sentence'" (Rev 16:5). Another angel has charge of fire: "Then another angel [came] from the altar, [who] was in charge of the fire, and cried out in a loud voice to the one who had the sharp sickle" (Rev 14:18). Four angels are assigned to the four winds: "After this I saw four angels standing at the four corners of

the earth, holding back the four winds of the earth so that no wind could blow on land or sea or against any tree" (Rev 7:1).

 The Old Testament idea of **angelic control of the elements and heavenly bodies**, like the biblical concept of God's heavenly court, has parallels in other Mesopotamian religions. In the Babylonian religion, for example, each of the seven visible planets was ruled by its own minor deity. Other spirits—such as the god Ishkur, who was believed to govern storms and rainfall—were thought to control forces of the natural world.

In other passages, angels are associated with stars. The book of Judges describes a battle between Israel and the Canaanite general, Sisera. The stars participate in this battle: "From the heavens the stars fought; / from their courses they fought against Sisera" (Judg 5:20). Stars can fight for Israel because they are understood not as inanimate matter but as angelic beings. The book of Job further recounts that when God created the world, "the morning stars sang together / and all the sons of God shouted for joy" (Job 38:7). Here Job envisions the angelic controllers of the stars singing together with the other angels in joy over God's establishment of the world.

The Bible, then, understands that angelic beings of God's court have been assigned to rule nations and the elements of the world. But the high position of these controlling angels carries with it an inherent danger: humans can be tempted to direct to angels the homage that belongs to God alone.

The Temptation to Worship Angels

The angels of the heavenly court were seen as glorious and powerful. It is no wonder, then, that throughout the Bible humans are tempted to worship them. The biblical authors make every attempt to subordinate these angelic beings to the one true God. There are, however, indications in the Scriptures that their efforts were not always successful.

Deuteronomy recognizes this perversion and warns against it: "And when you look up to the heavens and behold the sun or the moon or the stars, the whole heavenly host, do not be led astray into bowing down to them and serving them. These the LORD, your God, has apportioned to all the other nations under the heavens" (Deut 4:19). Later in the same book, sin is described as the false worship of angels: "going to serve other gods, by bowing down to them, to the sun or the moon or any of the host of heaven, contrary to my command" (Deut 17:3). This action is described as a transgression of God's covenant (17:2).

The book of Wisdom also recognizes the lure to worship angels. The author argues that angels are only creatures and that God is more worthy of human homage:

Wisdom 13:2-4

²Instead either fire, or wind, or the swift air,
    or the circuit of the stars, or the mighty
        water,
    or the luminaries of heaven, the governors
        of the world, they considered gods.
³Now if out of joy in their beauty they
        thought them gods,
    let them know how far more excellent is
        the Lord than these;
    for the original source of beauty
        fashioned them.
⁴Or if they were struck by their might and
        energy,
    let them realize from these things how
        much more powerful is the one
        who made them.

The New Testament testifies that the worship of angels remained a danger for the early church. The author of the letter to the Colossians warns that some in the community were inclined to follow "an empty, seductive philosophy according to human tradition" (Col 2:8). This philosophy is said to include the worship of angels:

Colossians 2:18-19

¹⁸Let no one disqualify you, delighting in self-abasement and worship of angels, taking his stand on visions, inflated without reason by his fleshly mind, ¹⁹and not holding closely to the head, from whom the whole body, supported and held together by its ligaments and bonds, achieves the growth that comes from God.

Some in the community at Colossae may have understood the worship of angels as an effective addition to faith in Christ, protecting them from evil cosmic powers. But the letter insists that such worship is opposed to true faith. Worshiping angels amounts to a denial of the sufficiency of Christ's saving work.

Another phrase in the New Testament likely also refers to controlling angels. The author of Colossians refers to "the elemental powers of this world" to describe a philosophy he opposes: "See to it that no one captivate you with an empty, seductive philosophy according to human tradition, according to the elemental powers of the world and not according to Christ" (Col 2:8). Later in the letter the author insists that these "elemental powers" are opposed to Christ: "If you died with Christ to the elemental powers of the world, why do you submit to regulations as if you were still living in the world?" (Col 2:20). Paul also speaks of "elemental powers" in Galatians 4:9, where again they are associated with past practices rather than new life in Christ: "[B]ut now that you have come to know God, or rather to be known by God, how can you turn back again to the weak and destitute elemental powers? Do you want to be slaves to them all over again?"

Scholars debate the meaning of "the elemental powers of the world." Should these powers be seen as the basic elements of creation or as a reference to the angelic powers that control them? A definitive resolution to this debate is impossible. The texts that use the phrase simply do not provide enough context for adequate interpretation. However, when we appreciate the widespread biblical belief in controlling angels, "the elemental powers of the world" can legitimately be interpreted as angelic powers—another way to name angelic forces guiding the structures of the world.

Contemporary Relevance: The temptation to worship angels might seem foreign and archaic to us as modern readers. The Christian tradition has long ago determined that angels are only creatures despite their glorious status. Therefore, we are not inclined to see them as semi-deities who in any way compete with God. Even though the idea of controlling angels is widespread in the New Testament, the church never made belief in such cosmic powers a part of faith. We are not expected to believe that God rules the cosmos through the agency of such spirits. Yet the ancient belief in controlling angels can still speak to us. Our world is shaped by ideas and powers, even if we do not envision them as angels. The things around us, nature and nations, do not only have a physical presence. They hold spiritual leverage over us. The biblical idea of controlling angels reminds us that there are powerful forces in our world that influence our lives. Such forces can be for good or ill. We are called to evaluate them in light of the gospel of Christ.

What are the "elemental powers" that structure our culture? Consumerism ranks high in first-world societies. Our lives are shaped by what we buy and want to buy. Consumerism can be good when it promotes jobs and supports a just economy. Consumerism can be destructive, however, when it becomes the primary means to achieve happiness or when our value as persons is equated with what we own. Being ruled by the social force "to possess" is a form of idolatry. It is worshiping "the angel of consumerism."

Individualism is another elemental power that can control us. Individualism is good when it supports the freedom and dignity of the person and spurs thought and creativity. But individualism becomes harmful when it focuses on "my good alone" and when any claim for the common good is negated by our own personal preferences. When the individual is exalted above all else, we worship "the angel of individualism."

Nationalism is another force that shapes our lives. Nationalism is good when it unites citizens in common efforts to promote a just society and spurs them to protect what is good. But nationalism becomes dangerous when it excludes some as full citizens because of race, heritage, or religion—or when it extols one nation as the norm to which all others must aspire. Such attitudes amount to idolatry, worshiping "the angel of nationalism."

The elemental powers of our world, angelic or otherwise, influence us and can control us. Their value must be judged in light of the supreme role of Christ. This is the conviction of the New Testament. It is to this conviction that we now turn.

Christ's Superiority to Angels: Hebrews

A major theme of the letter to the Hebrews is the superiority of Christ to all creatures. Much is debated about this ancient letter, including its author and when it was written. But there is no doubt that this letter asserts the primacy of Christ as Son and High Priest. As the letter begins, the author stresses that Christ is superior to the angels. Why this emphasis? Perhaps, like the church at Colossae, some recipients of this letter were tempted to worship angels. Perhaps some readers were identifying Christ himself as an angel, thereby compromising his unique status. Whatever the reason, the first verses of the letter proclaim Christ's superiority over angelic beings: "When he had accomplished purification from sins, / he took his seat at the right hand of the Majesty on high, / as far superior to the angels / as the name he has inherited is more excellent than theirs" (Heb 1:3-4).

Hebrews regularly uses passages from the Old Testament to demonstrate its claims concerning Jesus. Immediately after the initial assertion that Jesus is superior to the angels, the author uses a series of biblical references to support his position. First, he cites Psalm 2:7 and 2 Samuel 7:14. Both of these passages originally referred to the king of Israel as God's son. Hebrews uses these passages to demonstrate the superior status of Christ over the angels: "For to which of the angels did God ever say: / 'You are my son; this day I have begotten you'? / Or again: / 'I will be a father to him, and he shall be a son to me?'" (Heb 1:5).

 Scholarly investigation of the book of Hebrews' emphasis on **Christ's superiority over the angels** has focused on Jewish beliefs popular in the first century that placed messianic hopes in angelic figures. Such beliefs were founded on readings of certain scriptural texts (see Exod 23:20; Mal 2:7; and Dan 12:1) that in turn led some sects of Judaism to ascribe eschatological, messianic significance to figures like the angel Michael and the mysterious priestly king Melchizedek (Gen 14:18).

The author then turns to Deuteronomy 32:43. He uses this text to show that far from being superior to Christ ("the first-born"), the angels worship him: "And again, when [God] leads the first-born into the world, he says: / 'Let all the angels of God worship him'" (Heb 1:6). The next quotation is from Psalm 104:4, which, as we have already seen, associates the angels with the controlling spirits of wind and flame. This association gives angels great dignity, but one that is passing. By contrast, the dignity of Jesus is associated with God's throne, which Psalm 45:7 says stands forever: "Of the angels [God] says: / 'He makes his angels

winds / and his ministers a fiery flame'; / but of the Son: / 'Your throne, O God, stands forever and ever; / and a righteous scepter is the scepter of your kingdom'" (Heb 1:7-8).

A few verses later, the author of Hebrews quotes Psalm 110:1. He applies this verse to Jesus who is seated at God's right hand. In a meal setting, the position at the host's right hand is the place of honor at table. No place is higher. Although angels are present at God's table, their role is secondary. In the same passage, the author also cites Psalm 91:11 (referring to angels as "ministering spirits"), arguing that the role of angels is to serve: "But to which of the angels has he ever said: / 'Sit at my right hand / until I make your enemies your footstool'? / Are they not all ministering spirits sent to serve, for the sake of those who are to inherit salvation?" (Heb 1:13-14). Jesus sits at the right hand of God. The angels only minister at God's table.

In chapter two the author of Hebrews takes his argument a step further. Referring to Psalm 8:5-7, he discusses how Jesus "for a little while" was made "lower than the angels" through his suffering and death. But the author is clear that Jesus is now crowned with glory and honor. Now he is superior to the angels:

Hebrews 2:5-8

⁵For it was not to angels that he subjected the world to come, of which we are speaking. ⁶Instead, someone has testified somewhere:
"What is man that you are mindful of him,
  or the son of man that you care for him?
⁷You made him for a little while lower than
    the angels;
  you crowned him with glory and honor,
⁸ subjecting all things under his feet."
In "subjecting" all things [to him], he left nothing not "subject to him." Yet at present we do not see "all things subject to him."

By employing this chorus of citations from the Hebrew Bible (Old Testament), the author of Hebrews bolsters his claim that there is no competition between Jesus and the angels. Jesus is the anointed Son who sits at the right hand of God. The angels are not.

Christ's Superiority to Angels: Ephesians, Colossians, and Philippians

Christ's dominance over angels is also asserted in the letter to the Ephesians.

Ephesians 1:18-23

18May the eyes of [your] hearts be enlightened, that you may know what is the hope that belongs to his call, what are the riches of glory in his inheritance among the holy ones, 19and what is the surpassing greatness of his power for us who believe, in accord with the exercise of his great might, 20which he worked in Christ, raising him from the dead and seating him at his right hand in the heavens, 21far above every principality, authority, power, and dominion, and every name that is named not only in this age but also in the one to come. 22And he put all things beneath his feet and gave him as head over all things to the church, 23which is his body, the fullness of the one who fills all things in every way.

Verse 21 is a crucial text for the study of angels. In it there are five words designating entities over which Christ rules. These entities are the controlling spirits of the world. The Greek words are translated differently in various English translations, but the most common translations are: principality (*arche*); authority (*exousia*); power (*dynamis*); dominion (*kyriotes*); and name (*onoma*). Ephesians asserts that through Christ's resurrection, Christ is exalted above all of these angelic realities. By stating that Christ is above these controlling spirits, Ephesians asserts that his position is higher than that of any creature.

The letter to the Colossians uses a similar grouping of names to state that all things were created through Christ:

Colossians 1:15-17

15He is the image of the invisible God,
    the firstborn of all creation.
16For in him were created all things in heaven
      and on earth,
    the visible and the invisible,
    whether thrones or dominions or
      principalities or powers;
    all things were created through him and
      for him.
17He is before all things,
    and in him all things hold together.

The visible and invisible things created through Christ are again enumerated with a set of titles (v. 16). When we compare these titles to those used in Ephesians 1:21, we note that "dominions," "principalities," and "powers" appear in both lists, while "authority" and "name" are missing in Colossians. We also note that in Colossians a new word, "thrones" (*thronos*), appears. All of these terms refer to the angelic beings who rule the cosmos. Whereas Ephesians used these terms to name the powers over which the risen Christ rules, Colossians employs them to show Christ's superiority from the very beginning of creation.

Paul also refers to angelic powers in his letter to the Philippians. Here he quotes an early Christological hymn that describes the status of Christ:

Philippians 2:5-11

5Have among yourselves the same attitude that is also yours in Christ Jesus,
6Who, though he was in the form of God,
    did not regard equality with God
      something to be grasped.

> 7 Rather, he emptied himself,
> taking the form of a slave,
> coming in human likeness;
> and found human in appearance,
> 8 he humbled himself,
> becoming obedient to death,
> even death on a cross.
> 9Because of this, God greatly exalted him
> and bestowed on him the name
> that is above every name,
> 10 that at the name of Jesus
> every knee should bend,
> of those in heaven and on earth and
> under the earth,
> 11 and every tongue confess that
> Jesus Christ is Lord,
> to the glory of God the Father.

According to this hymn, Christ is exalted by the Father above every other reality. He has received the name that is above every name (v. 9). In the Bible a name is an expression of the person's very being. Jesus Christ is named as "Lord" to identify his exalted state. He is "above every name." But "name" here also identifies an angelic power. "Name" (*onoma*) is the title of a controlling spirit of the cosmos. The scope of such angelic powers is emphasized in verse 10 where Paul talks of every knee bending: "of those in heaven and on earth and under the earth." Similar to the claim in Colossians 1:16 that Jesus is superior to "all things in heaven and on earth, / the visible and the invisible," Philippians asserts that Jesus has been exalted above every material and angelic being.

 The Angelic Hierarchy in the Tradition and Liturgy

Although Paul and other New Testament writers frequently refer to angelic powers, they do not pause to explain to us who these spirits are or over what elements they rule. There is no effort in the New Testament to explain the functions of angelic forces or to organize them in any way. After the New Testament era, believers longed to know more about the order and classification of angels. They searched the Scriptures to locate names by which they could arrange angels into groupings. Ephesians and Colossians proved an essential source for such endeavors.

Drawing upon biblical terms, various "choirs" were suggested to form a hierarchy of angels praising God. By the fourth century, the developing tradition settled on nine angelic choirs. This arrangement was reached by assigning angels into three ranks of three. The Seraphim and Cherubim were placed together with the "Thrones" of Colossians in the first rank. Dominions, Virtues (from the Greek *dynamis* or "powers"), and Powers (from the Greek *exousia* or "authority") comprised the second rank. Principalities were then placed with Archangels and the generic word "Angels" to form the lowest rank.

Christians today most often encounter these "choirs of angels" in worship. The Catholic liturgy employs a preface before the eucharistic prayer. Each preface invites us to join the angels in praise of God. In many prefaces, the reference to angels is a general one, as in the Third Common Preface: *"[W]e, too, extol you with all the Angels, / as in joyful celebration we acclaim . . ."* But the names of angelic groups are sometimes specifically mentioned, as in the First Common Preface: *"And so, with Angels and Archangels, / with Thrones and Dominions, / and with all the hosts and Powers of heaven, / we sing the hymn of your glory, / as without end we acclaim . . ."* Occasionally another listing of angelic choirs including the Seraphim is used, as in the First Preface of the Blessed Virgin Mary: *"[T]he Angels praise your majesty, / Dominions adore and Powers tremble before you. / Heaven and the Virtues of heaven and the blessed Seraphim / worship together with exultation. / May our voices, we pray, join with theirs / in humble praise, as we acclaim . . ."*

The use of angelic groupings in the eucharistic prefaces imitates the biblical practice of using a selection of controlling spirits to represent all that exists. All that has been created and all that has been redeemed joins in the praise of God.

Contemporary Relevance: It is worth noting why Paul quotes this early hymn about Christ. He encourages his readers, "Have among yourselves the same attitude that is also yours in Christ Jesus" (v. 5). What is the attitude he wishes the Philippians to imitate? Although the hymn describes Christ's glory, it also tells how he attained it. It was not by striving to be like God (v. 6) but by humbling himself to take up "the form of a slave" and by accepting death on a cross (v. 8). Christ did not attain the highest position by aiming for it. Rather, it was through acceptance of his human state and the suffering it involved that he was exalted by God (vv. 9-11). Paul calls the Philippians to imitate that humility. Immediately before he quotes the hymn, Paul makes this point explicitly: "Do nothing out of selfishness or out of vainglory; rather, humbly regard others as more important than yourselves, each looking out not for his own interests, but [also] everyone for those of others" (Phil 2:3-4).

"Selfishness" and "vainglory" are a constant temptation for us. As we live our lives, we can find ourselves aiming not for the good but rather for recognition that we are good. We can make choices based not on what will truly make a difference but on what will impress others. This passage tells us that the way to glory is through humility. A mother succeeds not when she is recognized as a "good mother" but when she works to understand her children and provide what they truly need. An employer does not flourish by striving to win accolades in the media but by listening to his or her employees and treating them justly. We do not reach the top when others admire our talents and virtues but when we stand with the weak and broken and see them as brothers and sisters.

Jesus has been exalted above every angelic power. Yet that glory has been reached through humility. It is when we humbly regard others as more important than ourselves that God will lift us up to share in the glory of Christ's reign.

Christ's Cosmic Victory

Angelic powers are employed not only to describe what God has already accomplished in Christ but also what God will accomplish in the future. The death and resurrection of Jesus is the first step in God's plan for the world. But the work of Christ has a cosmic extension. Christ died and rose not only for individual Christians but for all creation. The fulfillment of Christian hope is not our personal arrival in heaven; rather heaven is where we wait for the final act of God that will take place when Christ returns in glory. On that day all on earth and all in heaven will be transformed by Christ into a new creation.

Paul makes this clear in his first letter to the Thessalonians. When Paul envisions Christ's triumphal return, he describes an angelic presence. The voice of an archangel announces the resurrection of the dead.

---

1 Thessalonians 4:16-17

[16]For the Lord himself, with a word of command, with the voice of an archangel and with the trumpet of God, will come down from heaven, and the dead in Christ will rise first. [17]Then we who are alive, who are left, will be caught up together with them in the clouds to meet the Lord in the air. Thus we shall always be with the Lord.

Paul assures the Thessalonians that on the last day, both those who have died and those who are still alive will be resurrected into a new existence with Christ. He is also clear that Christ's final victory will not be limited to humans—all creation will share in it. Paul asserts this dramatically in the following passage from Romans.

> *Romans 8:18-23*
>
> [18]I consider that the sufferings of this present time are as nothing compared with the glory to be revealed for us. [19]For creation awaits with eager expectation the revelation of the children of God; [20]for creation was made subject to futility, not of its own accord but because of the one who subjected it, in hope [21]that creation itself would be set free from slavery to corruption and share in the glorious freedom of the children of God. [22]We know that all creation is groaning in labor pains even until now; [23]and not only that, but we ourselves, who have the firstfruits of the Spirit, we also groan within ourselves as we wait for adoption, the redemption of our bodies.

It is not only individual Christians who await Christ's glorious return: "All creation is groaning in labor pains" (v. 22). All created reality is destined to share in Christ's final victory. The plan of God is to transform our world into a new creation in which God's will holds sway over all things. The resurrection of Jesus has already taken place, and Christ sits at God's right hand. But Paul explains that Christ's final victory is yet to come. He gives us a clear timeline in 1 Corinthians 15.

> *1 Corinthians 15:22-28*
>
> [22]For just as in Adam all die, so too in Christ shall all be brought to life, [23]but each one in proper order: Christ the firstfruits; then, at his coming, those who belong to Christ; [24]then comes the end, when he hands over the kingdom to his God and Father, when he has destroyed every sovereignty and every authority and power. [25]For he must reign until he has put all his enemies under his feet. [26]The last enemy to be destroyed is death, [27]for "he subjected everything under his feet." But when it says that everything has been subjected, it is clear that it excludes the one who subjected everything to him. [28]When everything is subjected to him, then the Son himself will [also] be subjected to the one who subjected everything to him, so that God may be all in all.

Using an agricultural image, Paul calls Jesus the "firstfruits" of what is to come (v. 23). In his resurrection Jesus is the first to be raised up, the "firstfruits" of the harvest. But we too are a part of the harvest and will be raised up. At his return we will share in his risen glory. Then at the end of all things, Christ will assert his power over "every sovereignty and every authority and power" (v. 24). We recognize in these words the biblical concept of the controlling angelic forces that govern this present world. Paul uses strong language here. He seems to be indicating that even the angelic forces must be destroyed. Regardless of how we understand this on a literal level, Paul is insisting that the present configuration of the world, which controlling angels support, must be undone and replaced by a new creation. Then every aspect of the new world will be subjected to Christ, and the Son himself will be subjected to the Father, so that "God may be all in all" (v. 28). The new creation will be one in which God's will is perfectly obeyed. It will be a world without evil or death (v. 26), a world in which every authority has been made subservient to the power of Christ.

Contemporary Relevance: We wait for the transformation of our world. But as we wait, the suffering and pain of our present world continues. Even as we look forward in hope to an existence in which God is all in all, we must still deal with the structures of our present existence which include violence, loss, and death. So how do we live in hope when so much of our experience is still under the sway of death? Paul addresses this question in one of the most powerful passages in the New Testament. In Romans 8 he assures us that whatever we must face, whatever may happen to us, Christ is still with us.

Romans 8:31-39

[31]What then shall we say to this? If God is for us, who can be against us? [32]He who did not spare his own Son but handed him over for us all, how will he not also give us everything else along with him? [33]Who will bring a charge against God's chosen ones? It is God who acquits us. [34]Who will condemn? It is Christ [Jesus] who died, rather, was raised, who also is at the right hand of God, who indeed intercedes for us. [35]What will separate us from the love of Christ? Will anguish, or distress, or persecution, or famine, or nakedness, or peril, or the sword? [36]As it is written:

"For your sake we are being slain all the day;
we are looked upon as sheep to be
slaughtered."

[37]No, in all these things we conquer overwhelmingly through him who loved us. [38]For I am convinced that neither death, nor life, nor angels, nor principalities, nor present things, nor future things, nor powers, [39]nor height, nor depth, nor any other creature will be able to separate us from the love of God in Christ Jesus our Lord.

Paul's words ring with confidence. God is for us (v. 31). God will give us all we need (v. 32). God acquits us of sin (v. 33). Christ intercedes for us (v. 34). No evil we experience can separate us from Christ's love (v. 35). We in fact are conquerors (v. 37). Paul then lists every "creature" that might render God's promise to us void. He includes life and death, the present and the future. He also includes angels, principalities, and powers (v. 38). Even though these controlling spirits still exercise authority in a world that is not yet in conformity to God's will, we need not fear their effects upon us. Christ's victory has already begun, and his love surrounds us. He holds the elemental powers of this world in check until the day when he will transform them into a new creation.

EXPLORING LESSON FOUR

1. How do scholars understand the cultural origins of the Bible's depiction of angels in the heavenly court?

_____

_____

_____

_____

_____

2. The Bible asserts that God appointed angels as controlling powers even of pagan countries (Deut 32:8-9). What is meant by the statement that this belief is "an emerging proclamation of the universal reign of God"? (See page 59.)

_____

_____

_____

_____

_____

3. While we do not think of "controlling angels" governing the elements of our world today, how might this ancient biblical idea still enlarge our appreciation of God's creation?

_____

_____

_____

_____

_____

4. Some Scripture passages warn against the worship of angels (e.g., Col 2:18-19; Heb 1:5-14). How might a warning against worshiping anything other than God still be appropriate for believers today?

_____

_____

_____

_____

_____

5. The author of Hebrews used complex quotations from the Old Testament to present his convictions (Heb 1:3-14). Although this style was very popular in the ancient world, it may be difficult to follow today. What was your experience? Did his technique help or hinder your understanding?

_____

_____

_____

_____

_____

6. Using the hymn of Christ's glorification in Philippians 2, Paul argues that we should follow Christ's way of humility. Do you feel that this way of humility can really "work" in a world so driven by personal success? Can you share any examples from your own life where the way of humility has led to success?

_____

_____

_____

_____

_____

7. Were you aware that many of the prefaces at the Catholic Eucharist use the titles of angels (see 🔥 on page 65)? Do you feel that being aware of such references during Mass might enhance your own prayer and worship? In what way?

_____

_____

_____

_____

_____

8. Explain in your own words what Paul describes in 1 Corinthians 15:22-28. How does Paul's description broaden your understanding of the purpose of Jesus' death and resurrection?

_____

_____

_____

_____

_____

9. Paul insists that nothing can separate us from the love of Christ (Rom 8:31-39). Reflect on Paul's words. Have they proven true in your life? How do you understand these words in a time when some of our Christian brothers and sisters have lost their faith because of suffering, calamities, or scandal?

_____

_____

_____

_____

_____

CLOSING PRAYER

Prayer

For the Lord himself, with a word of command, with the voice of an archangel and with the trumpet of God, will come down from heaven, and the dead in Christ will rise first. Then we who are alive, who are left, will be caught up together with them in the clouds to meet the Lord in the air. Thus we shall always be with the Lord. (1 Thess 4:16-17)

Lord Jesus, give us the wisdom to understand and the faith to believe that the tribulations of this world will be swept away forever when you come again in glory. May our knowledge of your ultimate victory be a source of hope and comfort as we journey through life. Our confidence in you gives us strength. Today may we use that strength to . . .

LESSON FIVE

Destroying Evil:
Angels as Ministers
of God's Judgment

Begin your personal study and group discussion with a simple and sincere prayer such as:

Prayer

God of heaven and earth, may our time of study and reflection lead us to imitate the angels as heralds of your word and proclaimers of your glory.

Read pages 74–86 , Lesson Five.

Respond to the questions on pages 87–89, Exploring Lesson Five.

The Closing Prayer on page 90 is for your personal use and may be used at the end of group discussion.

DESTROYING EVIL: ANGELS AS MINISTERS OF GOD'S JUDGMENT

Angels do what God does. We should therefore not be surprised to discover that angels in the Bible are ministers of God's judgment. Passing judgment was an essential characteristic of all gods of the ancient Near East. Issuing decrees and verdicts from which there was no appeal was a sure sign of divine power. The God of Israel was no exception. Throughout the Bible, God is presented as a powerful judge.

The psalms, for example, often cry out for God's judgment. Psalm 26:1-3 declares:

¹Judge me, Lord!
    For I have walked in my integrity.
In the Lord I trust;
    I do not falter.
²Examine me, Lord, and test me;
    search my heart and mind.
³Your mercy is before my eyes;
    I walk guided by your faithfulness.

Psalm 43:1-2 begs for God's judgment against those who oppress the psalmist:

¹Grant me justice, O God;
    defend me from a faithless people;
    from the deceitful and unjust rescue me.
²You, O God, are my strength.
    Why then do you spurn me?
Why must I go about mourning,
    with the enemy oppressing me?

When David refuses to attack Saul during their contest for kingship, he assures Saul that the outcome of their struggle will be determined not by his actions but by the judgment of God: "May the Lord judge between me and you. May the Lord exact justice from you in my case. I shall not lay a hand on you" (1 Sam 24:13).

Although God is often shown to execute judgment directly, angels frequently act as mediators. Psalm 35:4-6 prays for a pursuing angel of judgment:

⁴Let those who seek my life
    be put to shame and disgrace.
Let those who plot evil against me
    be turned back and confounded.
⁵Make them like chaff before the wind,
    with the angel of the Lord driving them on.
⁶Make their way slippery and dark,
    with the angel of the Lord pursuing them.

In the Bible, God's judgment is identified with justice. God is not simply a judge who decides, but a judge who decides with righteousness. Unlike the gods of other nations who might pass judgment based on a particular influence or whim, the God of Israel judges in order to bring about what is right. Psalm 36:7 equates God's judgment and justice: "Your justice is like the highest mountains; / your judgments, like the mighty deep; / human being and beast you sustain, Lord." Psalm 94:14-15 asserts that when God is present, judgment is just: "For the Lord will not forsake his people, / nor abandon his inheritance. / Judgment shall again be just, / and all the upright of heart will follow it."

Many Christians struggle with the notion of God as a judge. They imagine an opposition between judgment and love. The first Christian heretic, Marcion, succumbed to this dichotomy.

In the second century, Marcion began to teach that there were two gods: the creator god of the Old Testament and the father of Jesus. The god of the Old Testament was a god of judgment, whereas the god of the New Testament was a god of love and mercy. According to Marcion, the purpose of Jesus' coming was to replace judgment with love. As a result, Marcion taught that the Old Testament was no longer valid for Christians. Marcion was excommunicated by the Church of Rome in 144 CE, but the residue of his teaching lingers to this day. Some Christians are still inclined to see the Old Testament as a "Bad Testament" of law and judgment. In contrast, the New Testament is embraced as a "Good Testament" in which God is loving and merciful.

Such a characterization of the Bible's two testaments, however, does not stand up to scrutiny. Anyone who reads the Bible in its entirety soon realizes that God's judgment and mercy pervade both the Old and the New Testaments. For example, the Old Testament contains some of the most beautiful and tender images of God's love. Isaiah 49:15 compares God's love to that of a mother: "Can a mother forget her infant, / be without tenderness for the child of her womb? / Even should she forget, / I will never forget you." Likewise, the New Testament includes passages of decisive judgment. In John 15:6 Jesus says, "Anyone who does not remain in me will be thrown out like a branch and wither; people will gather them and throw them into a fire and they will be burned."

God's judgment and God's love are not opposed to each other. In its deepest sense, the judgment of God is meant to promote what is good. Evil is a reality of our world, and God's judgment is directed against it.

Nevertheless, from a human perspective, identifying what is good and what is evil is not always clear. Many of the Scripture passages that we will discuss in this lesson portray moral choices in a simplistic manner that may offend modern sensibilities. As we examine the various ways God executes judgment through angelic ministers, we will note a wide range of nuance. Some presentations of God's judgment will seem primitive and one-dimensional. Others will surprise us with their remarkable sophistication and depth of insight.

Angels Judging Israel's Enemies

Evil is easily identified in circumstances of aggression. Oppressors who violently move against a person or nation are quickly recognized as mortal threats. In many passages of the Bible, God passes judgment against Israel's enemies in battle. In Judges 11:27, Jephthah writes to the king of the Ammonites as they prepare for battle. He understands it is God who will decide the outcome: "As for me, I have not sinned against you, but you wrong me by making war against me. Let the LORD, who is judge, decide this day between the Israelites and the Ammonites!"

During the time of the Jewish monarchy, the biblical writers presumed that God would support the king in his battles to defend the nation. 1 Samuel 2:10 declares: "The LORD's foes shall be shattered; / the Most High in heaven thunders; / the LORD judges the ends of the earth. / May he give strength to his king, / and exalt the horn of his anointed!" In Psalm 110:5-6, God is pictured at the right hand of the king, determining the outcome of battle: "At your right hand is the Lord, / who crushes kings on the day of his wrath, / Who judges nations, heaps up corpses, / crushes heads across the wide earth."

Second Kings also describes God's judgment against the Assyrian King, Sennacherib. Sennacherib laid siege to Jerusalem in 701 BCE. A deadly plague then wiped out most of his army and forced him to return home. Second Kings presents this plague as the work of the angel of the Lord:

2 Kings 19:32-36

[32]"Therefore, thus says the LORD about the king:

He shall not come as far as this city,
 nor shoot there an arrow,
 nor confront it with a shield,
Nor cast up a siege-work against it.
[33]By the way he came he shall leave,
 never coming as far as this city,
 oracle of the LORD.
[34]I will shield and save this city
 for my own sake and the sake of David my
 servant."

[35]That night the angel of the LORD went forth and struck down one hundred and eighty-five thousand men in the Assyrian camp. Early the next morning, there they were, dead, all those corpses! [36]So Sennacherib, the king of Assyria, broke camp, departed, returned home, and stayed in Nineveh.

In the book of Daniel, Nebuchadnezzar, King of Babylon, receives a dream in which an angel (here presented as "a holy watcher") announces God's judgment upon him. Daniel describes the dream and its meaning in the following passage:

Daniel 4:20-22

[20]"As for the king's vision of a holy watcher, who came down from heaven and proclaimed: 'Cut down the tree and destroy it, but leave its stump in the earth. Bound with iron and bronze, let him be fed with the grass of the field, and bathed with the dew of heaven; let his lot be with wild beasts till seven years pass over him'— [21]here is its meaning, O king, here is the sentence that the Most High has passed upon my lord king: [22]You shall be cast out from human society and dwell with wild beasts; you shall be given grass to eat like an ox and be bathed with the dew of

heaven; seven years shall pass over you, until you know that the Most High is sovereign over human kingship and gives it to whom he will."

Daniel 4:20 contains the first scriptural reference to angels as **"watchers" or "sentinels."** The use of this descriptor may be based on the image of angels found in Ezekiel 1:6, where each angel is described as having four distinct faces, allowing the angelic beings to "watch" in four directions at once. In light of the use of this term in Daniel, many commentators interpret the "sentinels" mentioned in Isaiah 62:6 as angelic beings, stationed on the walls of Jerusalem, who continually remind God of the divine promise to restore the city ("Upon your walls, Jerusalem, / I have stationed sentinels; / By day and by night, / they shall never be silent. / You who are to remind the Lord, / take no rest . . ."). "Watchers" also became a common term to describe angels in later apocryphal texts such as 1 Enoch.

Two final examples come from the story of the Exodus from Egypt, the defining moment of Israel's history. This supreme event of liberation is celebrated in the Bible's prose, poetry, and song. God judges the Egyptians directly in many accounts of the Exodus. But in several places, the mediation of an angel is indicated. Psalm 78:49-50 describes the plagues of Egypt and recognizes the activity of angels: "He let loose against them the heat of his anger, / wrath, fury, and distress, / a band of deadly messengers. / He cleared a path for his anger; / he did not spare them from death, / but delivered their animals to the plague." God's anger, wrath, fury, and distress are an angelic "band of deadly messengers" executing judgment on Egypt.

The last plague of Egypt was the death of Egypt's firstborn children. Exodus 12:23 indicates that this plague was the work of a destroying angel: "For when the LORD goes by to strike down the Egyptians, seeing the blood on the lintel and the two doorposts, the LORD will pass over that door and not let the destroyer come into your houses to strike you down." The "destroyer" mentioned in this passage is best understood as a destroying angel executing God's judgment. Hebrews 11:28 also refers to this angelic "destroyer" when describing the work of Moses: "By faith he kept the Passover and sprinkled the blood, that the Destroyer of the firstborn might not touch them."

A verdict against Israel's enemies is often delivered by an angel. But angels are also active when Israel itself is the object of God's judgment.

Angels Judging Israel

God's judgment is just, advancing against every evil, even when the evil is perpetrated by Israel. In these situations, angels sometimes render God's judgment. The book of Ezekiel, for example, refers to angels that judge Israel's sin. Ezekiel's vision of God's throne with the cherubim was already discussed in Lesson Two. Ezekiel 8–11 describes God's judgment against Jerusalem. In 8:1-18, Ezekiel is taken by an angel to receive a divine vision of what is to come. The angel ("a figure that looked like a man") takes Ezekiel to the place where "the statue of jealousy that provokes jealousy" stands (8:2-3). This statue is an idol, possibly of the god Asherah that King Manasseh had set up for worship (see 2 Kgs 21:7). The statue identifies the sin of Israel as idolatry, the worship of foreign gods. The angel shows Ezekiel how the elders have placed "figures of all kinds of creeping things and loathsome beasts" in the courtyard of the temple (8:7-13), how women at the north gate weep in worship of the god Tammuz (8:14-15), and how men in the inner court of the temple bow to the sun in worship (8:16-18).

Then the angel calls the "scourges of the city" to come. These are "six men," each with a weapon of destruction in his hand, and "[i]n their midst was a man dressed in linen, with a scribe's case at his waist" (Ezek 9:1-2). All of these characters are angels of judgment. God gives the following directions to the angel dressed in linen:

Ezekiel 9:4-7

[4][A]nd the LORD said to him: Pass through the city, through the midst of Jerusalem, and mark an X on the foreheads of those who grieve and lament over all the abominations practiced within it. [5]To the others he said in my hearing: Pass through the city after him and strike! Do not let your eyes spare; do not take pity. [6]Old and young, male and female, women and children—wipe them out! But do not touch anyone marked with the X. Begin at my sanctuary. So they began with the elders who were in front of the temple. [7]Defile the temple, he said to them, fill its courts with the slain. Then go out and strike in the city.

As the slaughter continues, God who sits on a moveable throne leaves Jerusalem (Ezek 11:22-23). God will not come again until the exiles in Babylon return and build a new temple. In the meantime, those who have worshiped the idols of Mesopotamia and Egypt are slain by God's scourging angels.

 The garb of the **"man dressed in linen"** (Ezek 9:2) recalls the apparel prescribed for priests in Exodus 28. This similarity in clothing may have suggested itself to the sacred writer since both priests and angels function as ministers of God. Some angels in later biblical passages are also described as being clothed in linen (Dan 10:5; 12:6; Rev 15:6; 19:14).

In another example, an angel executes divine judgment against King David. When David sins against God by conducting a forbidden census of the people, God offers three options for punishment. The prophet Gad lists these for David:

---

2 Samuel 24:13-17

[13]Gad then went to David to inform him. He asked: "Should three years of famine come upon your land; or three months of fleeing from your enemy while he pursues you; or is it to be three days of plague in your land? Now consider well: what answer am I to give to him who sent me?" [14]David answered Gad: "I am greatly distressed. But let us fall into the hand of God, whose mercy is great, rather than into human hands." [15]Thus David chose the plague. At the time of the wheat harvest it broke out among the people. The LORD sent plague over Israel from morning until the time appointed, and from Dan to Beer-sheba seventy thousand of the people died. [16]But when the angel stretched forth his hand toward Jerusalem to destroy it, the LORD changed his mind about the calamity, and said to the angel causing the destruction among the people: Enough now! Stay your hand. The angel of the LORD was then standing at the threshing floor of Araunah the Jebusite. [17]When David saw the angel who was striking the people, he said to the LORD: "It is I who have sinned; it is I, the shepherd, who have done wrong. But these sheep, what have they done? Strike me and my father's family!"

This is a troubling narrative. It portrays a simplistic view of God's judgment. David and his people are treated as one. Even though the sin was his, his people suffer the punishment. Seventy thousand of them die! We might hope for a more precise exercise of God's judgment, but this passage ignores our concerns. Nevertheless, several parts of the narrative hint at a more nuanced perspective. David chooses to place his future in God's hands, believing in God's mercy (v. 14). That mercy is partially realized when God stops the destructive angel from destroying Jerusalem (v. 16). David himself objects to the sweeping scope of judgment, pleading with God that the punishment should not affect the whole nation (v. 17). Although the understanding of God's judgment in this story is primitive, the biblical author is anticipating a more advanced perspective.

Exodus makes an initial move in that direction. A judging angel is sent to punish those who worshiped the golden calf on Mount Sinai:

Exodus 32:30-34

[30]On the next day Moses said to the people, "You have committed a grave sin. Now I will go up to the LORD; perhaps I may be able to make atonement for your sin." [31]So Moses returned to the LORD and said, "Ah, this people has committed a grave sin in making a god of gold for themselves! [32]Now if you would only forgive their sin! But if you will not, then blot me out of the book that you have written." [33]The LORD answered Moses: Only the one who has sinned against me will I blot out of my book. [34]Now, go and lead the people where I have told you. See, my angel will go before you. When it is time for me to punish, I will punish them for their sin.

The angelic judgment in this passage is less global than the judgment levelled against David. Only those who have actually sinned will receive the punishment of God.

Contemporary Relevance: The biblical passages of judgment which we have examined so far in this lesson are likely to raise a series of questions. Do Ammonites and other enemies of Israel deserve to die simply because they are on the wrong side of the battle? Should an entire city suffer because of the sin of its king? Does the freedom of Israel justify the killing of Egyptian children? Can all idolaters be effectively grouped together and slaughtered by avenging angels? Can those who avoid idolatry be easily identified by having an "X" on their foreheads? We strain against these simplistic presentations of God's judgment.

We might imagine that only modern believers raise such concerns, but the violent and simplistic manner in which God's judgment is portrayed in many biblical passages has been challenged by believers long before us. For example, as the Jewish rabbis of later centuries interpreted the stories of the Exodus, they wondered about God's attitude towards the Egyptians who drowned in the Red Sea. They offered the following story to express God's disposition:

> Before the crossing of the sea there was a heavenly debate over how the Egyptians should be treated. The angel of Egypt wanted God to deal with them in His attribute of divine compassion. Other angels, led by Michael and Gabriel, urged God to act with His attribute of strict justice. God agreed to act in strict justice, and the Egyptians drowned. When this happened the angels of heaven started to break out into song. But they were silenced by God Himself. "This is no time to sing when My creatures, human beings whom I made, are drowning!" This rebuke from God brought the angels to a halt before they could begin their singing. (*Sanhedrin 39b*)

This rabbinic story is meant to challenge the simplistic view of God's justice which at times appears in the Bible. Yes, God fought for Israel against the Egyptians. But the Egyptians too were created and loved by God.

The Judgment of Sodom: Two Perspectives

The destruction of Sodom in the book of Genesis counters an overly simplistic understanding of God's judgment. The story of Sodom is told in two narratives, each with dramatically different viewpoints. One narrative is the continuation of the story discussed in Lesson One: the announcement of Isaac's birth. After Sarah's laugh, Abraham's three visitors set out towards Sodom (Gen 18:16). By the time they reach the city, only two visitors, clearly identified as angels, remain. They meet Lot and dine with him (Gen 19:1-3). But the people of Sodom demand that Lot turn over the visitors to them so that they can abuse them. The angels strike those who wish to hurt them with a blinding light that frustrates their intentions (Gen 19:4-11). The angels then tell Lot and his family to flee the city saying, "We are about to destroy this place, for the outcry reaching the LORD against those here is so great that the LORD has sent us to destroy it" (Gen 19:13). Lot flees, and the destruction of Sodom occurs in Genesis 19:24-25: "[A]nd the LORD rained down sulfur upon Sodom and Gomorrah, fire from the LORD out of heaven. He overthrew those cities and the whole Plain, together with the inhabitants of the cities and the produce of the soil."

God's judgment on Sodom is fierce and complete. The violence of the destruction, however, does not go unchallenged. The purpose of the second narrative concerning Sodom is to question God's action. This narrative is found in Genesis 18:17-33. Because its viewpoint differs so greatly from the account in chapter 19, it seems likely that it was composed by another author and inserted before chapter 19 to serve as a criticism of it.

In Genesis 18:22-33, Abraham bargains with God over the fate of Sodom. Because it is among the most amazing passages in the Bible, it is worth considering in full.

Genesis 18:22-33

Abraham Intercedes for Sodom. [22]As the men turned and walked on toward Sodom, Abraham remained standing before the LORD. [23]Then Abraham drew near and said: "Will you really sweep away the righteous with the wicked? [24]Suppose there were fifty righteous people in the city; would you really sweep away and not spare the place for the sake of the fifty righteous people within it? [25]Far be it from you to do such a thing, to kill the righteous with the wicked, so that the righteous and the wicked are treated alike! Far be it from you! Should not the judge of all the world do what is just?" ²⁶The LORD replied: If I find fifty righteous people in the city of Sodom, I will spare the whole place for their sake. ²⁷Abraham spoke up again: "See how I am presuming to speak to my Lord, though I am only dust and ashes! ²⁸What if there are five less than fifty righteous people? Will you destroy the whole city because of those five?" I will not destroy it, he answered, if I find forty-five there. ²⁹But Abraham persisted, saying, "What if only forty are found there?" He replied: I will refrain from doing it for the sake of the forty. ³⁰Then he said, "Do not let my Lord be angry if I go on. What if only thirty are found there?" He replied: I will refrain from doing it if I can find thirty there. ³¹Abraham went on, "Since I have thus presumed to speak to my Lord, what if there are no more than twenty?" I will not destroy it, he answered, for the sake of the twenty. ³²But he persisted: "Please, do not let my Lord be angry if I speak up this last time. What if ten are found there?" For the sake of the ten, he replied, I will not destroy it.

³³The LORD departed as soon as he had finished speaking with Abraham, and Abraham returned home.

There is no other passage like this in the Bible. Abraham takes God to task. Although he does it very respectfully, Abraham disputes God's judgment. Verse 22 sets up the conversation, saying, "Abraham remained standing before the LORD." However, the earliest Hebrew text of this verse reads: "The LORD remained standing before Abraham." It seems that the original text was altered by later scribes who thought it inappropriate for God to stand before the judgment of Abraham. But that is exactly what happens in this passage. God is placed in the witness box to defend his actions.

As the scene unfolds, Abraham questions the justice of God's judgment. He is arguing that God should not destroy Sodom. He does this carefully, in a cajoling manner: "Far be it from you to do such a thing, to kill the righteous with the wicked. . . . Should not the

judge of all the world do what is just?" (v. 25). Abraham calls on God to show mercy. His words undercut biblical passages in which God's judgment appears cruel and unfair. It is as though Abraham is saying: "I think you are a much better God than the one described in many passages of the Bible."

This story implies that God is, in fact, that "much better God." Abraham's strategy inverts the usual approach to judgment. Instead of asking how many evil people in a city would justify its destruction, he asks how many good people are needed to save it. In a mathematical pattern that is almost comical as it shrinks smaller and smaller, Abraham pushes God to the wall. How many good people can save a city? Let's start with fifty, then forty-five, then forty, then thirty, then twenty, then ten. In even the most corrupt city, one can certainly find ten just people! When we come to this point in the narrative, we can appreciate Abraham's accomplishment. He has, in effect, convinced God never to destroy *any city* due to judgment of the sin within it.

God does not object to Abraham's bold and manipulative method. God allows Abraham's aggressive doggedness, consenting to each diminishing number. When God agrees to save the city if there are ten good people in it, the story does not dare to go further. But its trajectory implies that God could be pushed to five, one, or even zero.

This text shows us God's heart. It tells us that when you put God on the stand, you discover that the simplistic exercise of divine judgment which is so often presented in the Bible is not necessarily what God prefers or ultimately adopts. God remains a God of justice, but this story argues that the full exercise of God's judgment is not adequately captured in many biblical stories.

Contemporary Relevance: Genesis 18:22-33 inserts a contrary voice into the biblical narrative. But it is not the final voice. In chapter 19, Sodom is still destroyed despite God's agreement with Abraham. By setting these two narratives side by side, the authors of Genesis create an unresolvable tension. One account states that God will not destroy Sodom. The other shows the city's destruction taking place through avenging angels. Such a tension reminds us that no biblical picture of God's judgment is definitive and that attempting to fully understand God's ways is as foolish as arguing numbers with Abraham.

Sodom and Gomorrah are destroyed. Yet the story of Abraham's remarkable conversation with God whispers to us: "Despite the way some biblical passages appear, God has no desire to harm the innocent or execute violence upon creation."

Angels of Judgment in the New Testament

Angels appear frequently in the New Testament as agents of God's judgment. But the judgment in question here is the judgment that will occur on the last day. The New Testament respects the timeline that we have already examined in 1 Corinthians 15:22-28 (Lesson Four): the resurrection of Christ has definitively begun the establishment of God's kingdom, but that kingdom will not be fully realized until Christ returns in glory. Salvation, then, is "already" and "not yet." The kingdom has already begun but is not yet complete. The New Testament focuses on the final judgment that will accompany Christ's return.

Today most Christians expect a judgment by God at the moment of their death (often called the "particular judgment"). Though now a clear part of Catholic teaching, this concept did not become a part of Christian belief until late in the medieval period. Judgment in the New Testament is understood as judgment on the last day. Angels are typically the agents of this final action of God.

This does not, however, prevent God from judging wicked individuals in the New Testament. The book of Acts presents the death of Herod Agrippa, the grandson of Herod the Great. God's judgment against him is executed by an angel as Herod addresses the people of Tyre and Sidon:

Acts 12:21-23

[21]On an appointed day, Herod, attired in royal robes, [and] seated on the rostrum, addressed them publicly. [22]The assembled crowd cried out, "This is the voice of a god, not of a man." [23]At once the angel of the Lord struck him down because he did not ascribe the honor to God, and he was eaten by worms and breathed his last.

This gruesome death of an individual, however, is an exception. In most cases angels are shown to accompany Christ as he comes to judge the world at the end of time. In Matthew 13:24-30, Jesus tells a parable about an enemy who scatters weeds among his neighbor's wheat. The neighbor decides to let both weeds and wheat grow together until harvest. Jesus explains the meaning of the parable as follows:

Matthew 13:36-43

[36]Then, dismissing the crowds, he went into the house. His disciples approached him and said, "Explain to us the parable of the weeds in the field." [37]He said in reply, "He who sows good seed is the Son of Man, [38]the field is the world, the good seed the children of the kingdom. The weeds are the children of the evil one, [39]and the enemy who sows them is the devil. The harvest is the end of the age, and the harvesters are angels. [40]Just as weeds are collected and burned [up] with fire, so will it be at the end of the age. [41]The Son of Man will send his angels, and they will collect out of his kingdom all who cause others to sin and all evildoers. [42]They will throw them into the fiery furnace, where there will be wailing and grinding of teeth. [43]Then the righteous will shine like the sun in the kingdom of their Father. Whoever has ears ought to hear.

The judgment of God in this passage is the judgment at the "end of the age" (v. 39). We are told that God will send his angels to separate "all who cause others to sin and all evildoers" (v. 41) from "the children of the kingdom" (vv. 38 and 43). Angels will be the ministers of the final judgment.

 Popular piety in the Middle Ages assigned a prominent role in the judgment of individuals to **the archangel Michael**. The source of this belief has its roots in Scripture: Jude 9 references the dispute between Michael and the devil over the deceased body of Moses, while a similar opposition between the two angelic powers in regard to Joshua is recounted in Zechariah 3:1-7. Medieval belief built on these references and eventually gave Michael specific functions in the personal and final judgments of individuals, including the role of intercessor and *psychopomp* (conductor of souls in their passage to heaven). Michael was also famously assigned the role of managing the *psychostasy*, or the "weighing" of individual souls. The origin of this last function, a frequent theme in medieval iconography, is not clear, but some scholars have noted a similarity to the ancient Egyptian religious belief that the hearts of those who died were weighed by the gods to determine their fate in the afterlife.

References to angels of God's judgment are also found in many of Jesus' sayings concerning the last day. Matthew's Gospel includes the following description of Christ's glorious return:

Matthew 24:29-31

²⁹"Immediately after the tribulation of those days,
the sun will be darkened,
and the moon will not give its light,
and the stars will fall from the sky,
and the powers of the heavens will be shaken.
³⁰And then the sign of the Son of Man will appear in heaven, and all the tribes of the earth will mourn, and they will see the Son of Man coming upon the clouds of heaven with power and great glory. ³¹And he will send out his angels with a trumpet blast, and they will gather his elect from the four winds, from one end of the heavens to the other.

A similar depiction is present in Matthew 16:27: "For the Son of Man will come with his angels in his Father's glory, and then he will repay everyone according to his conduct." Mark 8:38 (cf. Luke 9:26) is comparable: "Whoever is ashamed of me and of my words in this faithless and sinful generation, the Son of Man will be ashamed of when he comes in his Father's glory with the holy angels."

In 2 Thessalonians 1:5-10, Paul also envisions angels participating in God's judgment on the last day:

2 Thessalonians 1:5-10

⁵This is evidence of the just judgment of God, so that you may be considered worthy of the kingdom of God for which you are suffering. ⁶For it is surely just on God's part to repay with afflictions those who are afflicting you, ⁷and to grant rest along with us to you who are undergoing afflictions, at the revelation of the Lord Jesus from heaven with his mighty angels, ⁸in blazing fire, inflicting punishment on those who do not acknowledge God and on those who do not obey the gospel of our Lord Jesus. ⁹These will pay the penalty of eternal ruin, separated from the presence of the Lord and from the glory of his power, ¹⁰when he comes to be glorified among his holy ones and to be marveled at on that day among all who have believed, for our testimony to you was believed.

Angelic Evil: Satan

Because we tend to see God's salvation in light of our own individual faith journeys, we may read New Testament passages on judgment too narrowly. We view judgment as a personal evaluation of our own sin or holiness. The New Testament authors certainly consider our personal actions and decisions to be important, but they situate God's judgment of an individual as part of God's larger judgment of the world. The victory of Christ is not meant merely to save individuals from their sins but to eradicate evil within all creation.

By the time of the New Testament, cosmic evil is clearly personified in the character of Satan. Satan first appears by name in the book of Job, where he is a member of God's court whose role is to accuse Job before God. In the New Testament, Satan is the leader of evil angelic forces. Although there are only traces of it in the canonical scriptures, there is a tradition that Satan was part of a group of angels who sinned and fell from glory. Jude 5-6 makes a passing reference to this tradition: "I wish to remind you, although you know all things, that [the] Lord who once saved a people from the land of Egypt later destroyed those who did not believe. The angels too, who did not keep to their own domain but deserted their proper dwelling, he has kept in eternal chains, in gloom, for the judgment of the great day." 2 Peter 2:4 reflects a similar tradition: "God did not spare the angels when they sinned, but condemned them to the chains of Tartarus and handed them over to be kept for judgment."

In the New Testament, the name "Satan" occurs thirty-five times, and "the devil" occurs thirty-two times. Satan tempts Jesus in Matthew 4:1-11, Mark 1:12-13, and Luke 4:1-13, making clear that Jesus' ministry is a confrontation with cosmic evil. Satan orchestrates Jesus' betrayal by Judas in Luke 22:3 and John 13:27. Jesus sees Satan as the ruler of the present world in John 12:31: "Now is the time of judgment on this world; now the ruler of this world will be driven out."

According to this New Testament perspective, there are cosmic angelic forces aligned with Satan. They control this world for the time being. Paul ascribes the death of Jesus to these "rulers of this age":

1 Corinthians 2:6-8

[6]Yet we do speak a wisdom to those who are mature, but not a wisdom of this age, nor of the rulers of this age who are passing away. [7]Rather, we speak God's wisdom, mysterious, hidden, which God predetermined before the ages for our glory, [8]and which none of the rulers of this age knew; for, if they had known it, they would not have crucified the Lord of glory.

The "rulers of this age" are the controlling spirits of this world. The author of Colossians insists that the end of these angelic principalities and powers has definitively begun through Christ's resurrection:

Colossians 2:13-15

[13]And even when you were dead [in] transgressions and the uncircumcision of your flesh, he brought you to life along with him, having forgiven us all our transgressions; [14]obliterating the bond against us, with its legal claims, which was opposed to us, he also removed it from our midst, nailing it to the cross; [15]despoiling the principalities and the powers, he made a public spectacle of them, leading them away in triumph by it.

Yet until Christ's return, there is a continual struggle against Satan and the angelic rulers of the cosmos, as we read in this passage from Ephesians:

> ### Ephesians 6:11-13
>
> [11]Put on the armor of God so that you may be able to stand firm against the tactics of the devil. [12]For our struggle is not with flesh and blood but with the principalities, with the powers, with the world rulers of this present darkness, with the evil spirits in the heavens. [13]Therefore, put on the armor of God, that you may be able to resist on the evil day and, having done everything, to hold your ground.

Contemporary Relevance: The Scripture passages above show us that the New Testament takes evil angelic forces seriously. Every Christian will have to decide how great a role he or she wishes to ascribe to Satan and his angelic minions. Yet every Christian should appreciate how the presence of evil angelic forces within the Bible reminds us that evil is larger and more complex than our personal sins and failings. There are systems of corruption that continue to diminish us and deaden our society. Racism, sexual abuse, neglect of the environment, and economic disparity, for example, are more than wicked individual inclinations or societal impulses. It is our consolation that however powerful such forces may be, Christ's power is greater. And we stand with Christ.

Angels Judge Cosmic Evil: The Book of Revelation

According to the New Testament, the return of Christ will destroy all evil and will finally establish God's kingdom. His triumph will conquer Satan and the angelic forces aligned with him, so that the primordial goodness of creation might be restored. This defeat of evil is portrayed vividly in the book of Revelation. The purpose of this book is expressed in its opening verse: "The revelation of Jesus Christ, which God gave to him, to show his servants what must happen soon" (Rev 1:1).

Revelation announces that God's destruction of evil in Christ is about to happen and we should wait for it in hope. Angelic forces of good and evil fill Revelation and are used to describe God's triumph.

The action within the book of Revelation moves from heaven to earth. First, a vision of the throne of God is given. The four living creatures around God's throne in Revelation 4:6-8 are modeled on the cherubim of Ezekiel (see Lesson Two). In Revelation 5, the living creatures and countless angels praise God and Christ who is the Lamb:

> ### Revelation 5:11-12
>
> [11]I looked again and heard the voices of many angels who surrounded the throne and the living creatures and the elders. They were countless in number, [12]and they cried out in a loud voice:
> "Worthy is the Lamb that was slain
> to receive power and riches, wisdom and strength,
> honor and glory and blessing."

Praise flows from God's throne, praise for what God is about to do. God is about to destroy evil definitively.

In order for evil to end, God's judgment must flow from heaven, and this judgment is frequently carried out by angels. Their actions are presented in groups of seven. In chapters 8–11, seven angels blow seven trumpets of judgment. The first angel sends hail and fire to destroy a third of the earth (8:7). The second angel hurls a burning mountain into the sea, turning a third of it into blood (8:8-9). The third angel directs a star to fall on a third of the rivers and springs, poisoning them (8:10-11). The fourth angel darkens a third of the sun, moon, and stars (8:12). The fifth angel sends locusts to harm those not marked as followers of the Lamb (9:1-11). The sixth angel releases four more angels who kill a third of the human race (9:13-21). When the seventh angel blows his trumpet, the kingdom of God is established (11:15-19).

The narrative of Revelation is circular. Scenes of judgment and victory are repeated several times. Another pattern of destruction and then victory occurs later in the book when seven angels empty seven bowls upon the earth (16:1-21). It is important to note that Revelation is not giving us a literal description of what will happen on the last day. It is using vivid, gruesome imagery to assert that the evil that characterizes our present world will be destroyed so that God's kingdom may come.

The destruction pictured in the sections of the seven trumpets and seven bowls concerns the material world. Revelation also imagines the destruction of evil in the spiritual world, presenting the defeat of Satan more than once. Michael and his angels defeat the dragon (Satan) and his angels:

Revelation 12:7-9

[7]Then war broke out in heaven; Michael and his angels battled against the dragon. The dragon and its angels fought back, [8]but they did not prevail and there was no longer any place for them in heaven. [9]The huge dragon, the ancient serpent, who is called the Devil and Satan, who deceived the whole world, was thrown down to earth, and its angels were thrown down with it.

On earth Satan is defeated again and imprisoned for a thousand years. Then he is released and defeated forever:

Revelation 20:1-10

[1]Then I saw an angel come down from heaven, holding in his hand the key to the abyss and a heavy chain. [2]He seized the dragon, the ancient serpent, which is the Devil or Satan, and tied it up for a thousand years [3]and threw it into the abyss, which he locked over it and sealed, so that it could no longer lead the nations astray until the thousand years are completed. After this, it is to be released for a short time.

[4]Then I saw thrones; those who sat on them were entrusted with judgment. I also saw the souls of those who had been beheaded for their witness to Jesus and for the word of God, and who had not worshiped the beast or its image nor had accepted its mark on their foreheads or hands. They came to life and they reigned with Christ for a thousand years. [5]The rest of the dead did not come to life until the thousand years were over. This is the first resurrection. [6]Blessed and holy is the one who shares in the first resurrection. The second death has no power over these; they will be priests of God and of Christ, and they will reign with him for [the] thousand years.

[7]When the thousand years are completed, Satan will be released from his prison. [8]He will go out to deceive the nations at the four corners of the earth, Gog and Magog, to gather them for battle; their number is like the sand of the sea. [9]They invaded the breadth of the earth and surrounded the camp of the holy ones and the beloved city. But fire came down from heaven and consumed them. [10]The Devil who had led them astray was thrown into the pool of fire and sulfur, where the beast and the false prophet were. There they will be tormented day and night forever and ever.

Contemporary Relevance: As we absorb the vivid scenes of Revelation, we can become distracted by the violence of the events that seem to multiply themselves throughout the narrative. But our focus should stay on what the book is communicating through these scenes: God's judgment destroys evil and ultimately leads to cosmic and eternal victory. In this scenario, the intervention of God's angels of judgment is the first step toward a new creation.

Revelation can be accused of repeating scenes of destruction too frequently. But its final description of Christ's victory in the following passage is undoubtedly one of the most powerful, comforting passages in the Bible:

> ### *Revelation 21:1-5*
>
> [1]Then I saw a new heaven and a new earth. The former heaven and the former earth had passed away, and the sea was no more. [2]I also saw the holy city, a new Jerusalem, coming down out of heaven from God, prepared as a bride adorned for her husband. [3]I heard a loud voice from the throne saying, "Behold, God's dwelling is with the human race. He will dwell with them and they will be his people and God himself will always be with them [as their God]. [4]He will wipe every tear from their eyes, and there shall be no more death or mourning, wailing or pain, [for] the old order has passed away."
>
> [5]The one who sat on the throne said, "Behold, I make all things new."

Angels do what God does, and God passes judgment against the evil that disfigures creation. This will happen most completely on the last day when Christ comes on the clouds of heaven escorted by all the angels. Then there will be judgment—but that judgment will lead to the transformation of all things. On that day, all things will be made new.

EXPLORING LESSON FIVE

1. Marcion's solution to the tension between God's mercy and God's judgment was to differentiate between the god of the Old Testament and the father of Jesus in the New Testament. What is problematic about this approach?

_____

_____

_____

_____

_____

2. In times of war, Israel believed that God would pass judgment against its enemies (Judg 11:27; 1 Sam 2:10; 2 Kgs 19:32-36). Do you think people today tend to see God on their side and against those they consider their enemies? What dangers can arise from this perspective?

_____

_____

_____

_____

_____

_____

3. a) Did the destroying angels in Ezekiel 8–9 and 2 Samuel 24:13-17 disturb you or challenge your view of God's judgment? In what way?

_____

_____

_____

_____

b) How would you explain the presence of such passages in the Bible?

_____

_____

_____

_____

_____

4. In what way might the conversation between Abraham and God in Genesis 18:22-33 help us understand the relationship between God's mercy and God's justice?

_____

_____

_____

_____

_____

5. a) How can we explain the presence in the Bible of two very different stories of the destruction of Sodom (Gen 18:22-23 and Gen 19)?

_____

_____

_____

_____

b) Why does the Bible preserve both accounts?

_____

_____

_____

_____

6. The angels of judgment in the New Testament are almost always angels of the final judgment of the world (Matt 13:36-43; 24:29-31). Do you find it helpful to reflect on this emphasis on the cosmos rather than the individual? What challenges or insights do you gain from this perspective?

_____

_____

_____

_____

_____

7. What significance do you find in Paul's emphasis in 1 Corinthians 2:6-8 that Jesus' death was caused by angelic rather than political powers?

_____

_____

_____

_____

_____

_____

8. Ephesians 6:12 says that our struggle is not with "flesh and blood" but with angelic powers. How might we understand this? What larger forces do we face as followers of Christ?

_____

_____

_____

_____

_____

9. This lesson suggests that judgment in the book of Revelation is the destruction of cosmic evil leading to cosmic victory. Explain in your own words what is meant by this statement. How does this view of Revelation help you understand the book and its sometimes violent imagery?

_____

_____

_____

_____

_____

10. After reviewing the biblical passages about angels of judgment in this lesson, do you think you have a better understanding of God's judgment in our world? Which biblical passages were most meaningful to you?

_____

_____

_____

_____

_____

CLOSING PRAYER

Prayer

As the men turned and walked on toward Sodom, Abraham remained standing before the LORD. *Then Abraham drew near and said: "Will you really sweep away the righteous with the wicked?"* (Gen 18:22-23)

Heavenly Father, sometimes we struggle to perceive your presence in our world, and sometimes we fail to understand your providence and plans. Like Abraham, we sometimes question your justice and your compassion. Today we ask that as your children, we may never lose trust in your mercy or faith in your love. We especially ask for the wisdom to . . .

LESSON SIX

Protecting God's Own:
Guardian Angels

Begin your personal study and group discussion with a simple and sincere prayer such as:

Prayer

> *God of heaven and earth, may our time of study and reflection lead us to imitate the angels as heralds of your word and proclaimers of your glory.*

Read pages 92–104 , Lesson Six.

Respond to the questions on pages 105–107, Exploring Lesson Six.

The Closing Prayer on page 107 is for your personal use and may be used at the end of group discussion.

PROTECTING GOD'S OWN: GUARDIAN ANGELS

The God who loves us protects us. In a world that includes many threats and evils, God's power surrounds and guards us. In the Bible, this sheltering presence of God is often mediated through angels.

In the Old Testament, God frequently sends a protecting angel to Israel. As the Israelites leave Egypt, God accompanies them in a column of cloud and fire (Exod 13:21). As they prepare to cross the Red Sea, that column is associated with an angel, who moves behind them to protect them from the Egyptian army: "The angel of God, who had been leading Israel's army, now moved and went around behind them. And the column of cloud, moving from in front of them, took up its place behind them, so that it came between the Egyptian army and that of Israel. And when it became dark, the cloud illumined the night; and so the rival camps did not come any closer together all night long" (Exod 14:19-20).

Later, as the Israelites approach the Promised Land, God sends an angel to guard them: "See, I am sending an angel before you, to guard you on the way and bring you to the place I have prepared. Be attentive to him and obey him. Do not rebel against him, for he will not forgive your sin. My authority is within him. If you obey him and carry out all I tell you, I will be an enemy to your enemies and a foe to your foes" (Exod 23:20-22).

When Moses and the Israelites arrive at Kadesh, they send a message to the King of Edom asking to pass through his territory. In that message they recount how it was an angel who led them out of Egypt: "When we cried to the LORD, he heard our cry and sent an angel who led us out of Egypt" (Num 20:16).

We also find references to the guarding presence of angels in the psalms (see Pss 34 and 91) and in four Old Testament stories. We will now examine these four narratives to see how angels act as guardians in the lives of Jacob, Elijah, Daniel, and Tobit.

Jacob's Guardian Angel

Genesis 48:8-20

[8]When Israel saw Joseph's sons, he asked, "Who are these?" [9]"They are my sons," Joseph answered his father, "whom God has given me here." "Bring them to me," said his father, "that I may bless them." [10]Now Israel's eyes were dim from age; he could not see well. When Joseph brought his sons close to him, he kissed and embraced them. [11]Then Israel said to Joseph, "I never expected to see your face again, and now God has allowed me to see your descendants as well!"

[12]Joseph removed them from his father's knees and bowed down before him with his face to the ground. [13]Then Joseph took the two, Ephraim with his right hand, to Israel's left, and Manasseh with his left hand, to Israel's right, and brought them up to him. [14]But Israel, crossing his hands, put out his right hand and laid it on the head of Ephraim, although he was the younger, and his left hand on the head of Manasseh, although he was the firstborn. [15]Then he blessed them with these words:

"May the God in whose presence
my fathers Abraham and Isaac walked,

The God who has been my shepherd
    from my birth to this day,
[16]The angel who has delivered me from all
    harm,
    bless these boys
That in them my name be recalled,
    and the names of my fathers, Abraham
      and Isaac,
And they may become teeming multitudes
    upon the earth!"
[17]When Joseph saw that his father had laid his right hand on Ephraim's head, this seemed wrong to him; so he took hold of his father's hand, to remove it from Ephraim's head to Manasseh's, [18]saying, "That is not right, father; the other one is the firstborn; lay your right hand on his head!" [19]But his father refused. "I know it, son," he said, "I know. That one too shall become a people, and he too shall be great. Nevertheless, his younger brother shall surpass him, and his descendants shall become a multitude of nations." [20]So he blessed them that day and said, "By you shall the people of Israel pronounce blessings, saying, 'God make you like Ephraim and Manasseh.'" Thus he placed Ephraim before Manasseh.

In chapter 48 of Genesis, Jacob is preparing for death. He is bedridden, and his eyesight is failing. His son Joseph brings his two sons, Manasseh and Ephraim, to his father for his blessing. The blessing in question is no mere gesture of love and affection. It is a solemn ritual in which Jacob accepts his grandsons as his heirs. They become the future of Israel. In the blessing (see vv. 15-16), Jacob speaks of an angel who has protected him throughout his life.

As beautiful as the words of this blessing are, the context in which they occur is even more profound. To appreciate that context, we must remember who Jacob was. Jacob's life was unorthodox and wild. He was a twin to his brother Esau, and the two fought in their mother's womb over who would be born first. Esau came forth from the womb first, but Jacob came out gripping his brother's heel (Gen 25:21-26). When they grew older, the younger Jacob tricked Esau into selling his birthright for some bread and lentil stew (Gen 25:27-34). When their father, Isaac, was dying, Jacob took advantage of his father's failing eyesight to impersonate Esau. His father blessed Jacob instead of Esau, bestowing the family inheritance upon the younger son (Gen 27:1-45). By right of birth, Jacob should have been second to Esau. But by trickery and deception, he became Israel, the father of the twelve tribes. His duplicity left a wake of disaster. He was hated by his brother, separated from his mother, and broke his father's heart. Yet for most of his life, Jacob took solace in the fact that he had won. He had used dishonesty and fraud to seize the rights of a firstborn son.

When Joseph brings his sons to Jacob on his deathbed, all these tricks and scams hang in the air. Now Jacob is asked to bless Manasseh and Ephraim, just as Isaac was asked to bless Esau and Jacob many years before. The blessing, as before, is meant to bestow primacy upon the firstborn.

Despite the careful setup by Joseph, Jacob crosses his hands, giving the blessing of the firstborn to Ephraim who was born second (v. 14). Joseph sees the mistake and protests that Jacob has placed his right hand on the wrong grandson (v. 18). But Jacob dismisses Joseph's correction, saying, "I know it, son. . . . I know" (v. 19).

What does Jacob know? Perhaps Jacob knows how to cause trouble. His entire life has been fueled by the conviction that he could advance himself by catching others off guard. His wit allowed him to take what belonged to others and use it for his own advantage. Maybe the sudden crossing of his hands is merely another gesture to throw things out of balance, a last move by the old trickster.

Yet Jacob might know something more. Perhaps Jacob knows his God. Looking back over his life, Jacob may be realizing that somehow all of his wily moves had become a part of God's plan. It may be dawning on Jacob that his crafty choices, which he believed were for his own purposes, were really for God's purposes. Close to death, he may now understand that his God was "crafty" as well and has led him right to the place God wanted him to be. Jacob had become Israel, the father of God's people. Although Jacob is as clever as they come, this scene may be where he realizes that God was even more clever and had created something beautiful and lasting out of the tawdry pieces of his life. The sudden crossing of Jacob's hands, then, may be a salute to the shrewd God who had outwitted him at every turn.

Or perhaps what Jacob knows is deeper still. Perhaps Jacob knows that he is loved. He realizes that the place he finds himself in his last days is more of a blessing than he could have imagined. In verse 11, we are reminded that Jacob believed that he had lost his favorite son, Joseph, for good. Now not only is Joseph with him, but he has grandsons as well. Perhaps Jacob's stunning insight is that God has been good to him despite his life of manipulation, that an angel has protected him regardless of his self-serving choices, that he has been blessed even though he was the stealer of blessings. Aware of how little he deserves it, Jacob may now know that it was because of God's favor to him that he became the privileged son. If this is the case, then Jacob's crossing of his hands is not a trick or a gesture to a God who has outmaneuvered him, but rather the imitation of the God who loves him. The unexpected blessing of Ephraim as the firstborn, then, is an expression of the free and inexplicable kind of love that God gave to Jacob so many years before.

Contemporary Relevance: We all could be better people. We all look back on decisions we would like to change, and we are aware of failings we would like to erase. The story of Jacob in Genesis 48 reminds us that God's love for us is stronger than our imperfections. Even if we fall to selfishness, prejudice, or negligence towards others, God remains devoted to us, sending his angel to deliver us from harm. We should, of course, make every effort to improve. But it might be more likely than we expect that our lives will flow like Jacob's. One day, as our end draws near, we may find ourselves looking back on a life riddled with mistakes yet blessed in ways that are overwhelming. And when others remark that we could have lived holier lives and progressed more than we have, we, like Jacob, will say, "I know it. I know . . . I know I could have done things better. But I also know that an angel has protected me and God has loved me in spite of myself."

 Just before his death, Jacob appears to speak of **two protectors** who have shielded and guided him throughout his life: God who has been his "shepherd," and the angel who has "delivered" him from all harm (Gen 15–16). Some commentators have suggested that both of these protectors are in fact aspects of God and that the distinct identities point to two particular ways that God demonstrates care for the human race: through providential care for the whole world (God), and through the protection and guidance of each individual (angel).

Elijah's Guardian Angel

If Jacob's angel protects him even in his imperfections, the angel sent to Elijah guards him from despair. The story in question takes place in 1 Kings 19:1-8. Elijah has just killed the prophets of Baal who were attempting to lure Israel away from the true God (1 Kgs 18:16-40). Baal was a Canaanite god, promoted by King Ahab and his wife Jezebel. When Jezebel hears of Elijah's actions, she swears to kill him. Elijah flees for his life.

---

1 Kings 19:1-8

[1]Ahab told Jezebel all that Elijah had done—that he had murdered all the prophets by the sword. [2]Jezebel then sent a messenger to Elijah

and said, "May the gods do thus to me and more, if by this time tomorrow I have not done with your life what was done to each of them." ³Elijah was afraid and fled for his life, going to Beer-sheba of Judah. He left his servant there ⁴and went a day's journey into the wilderness, until he came to a solitary broom tree and sat beneath it. He prayed for death: "Enough, LORD! Take my life, for I am no better than my ancestors." ⁵He lay down and fell asleep under the solitary broom tree, but suddenly a messenger touched him and said, "Get up and eat!" ⁶He looked and there at his head was a hearth cake and a jug of water. After he ate and drank, he lay down again, ⁷but the angel of the LORD came back a second time, touched him, and said, "Get up and eat or the journey will be too much for you!" ⁸He got up, ate, and drank; then strengthened by that food, he walked forty days and forty nights to the mountain of God, Horeb.

There is a sudden shift in this story. In verse 3 Elijah flees from Jezebel to save his life, but in verse 4 he prays to God to end his life. Elijah moves from fear to despair. The truth of this narrative is that fear can turn into depression. Elijah comes to the conclusion that he can no longer be God's prophet. This is why he leaves his servant behind (v. 3) and simply walks out without a destination into the wilderness (v. 4). Despite his immense victory against the prophets of Baal on Mount Carmel, the power of the king and queen still control him. Ahab and Jezebel are too powerful to defeat, and Elijah is without hope. He sits beneath a broom tree and prays for death. God sends an angel to protect Elijah in his vulnerable condition.

Contemporary Relevance: This story addresses an extreme human situation that some of us may unfortunately have to face. The issue is not simply dissatisfaction or struggle but profound despair. Such loss of hope might arise from the collapse of our economic resources, the death of a loved one, or the diagnosis of a fatal disease. We lose the ability to continue. We succumb to hopelessness and wait for death. There is no easy escape from such darkness. But Elijah's story offers insights on how hope might be rekindled. Let's consider three of them.

1) *Hope responds to touch.* The angel sent to Elijah speaks to him, but first he *touches* him (vv. 5 and 7). Words alone are often not enough to penetrate the thick walls surrounding a person in despair. The logic and meaning that words convey may appear too weak to counter the weight of depression. Human touch has more power. Whether a gentle kiss from a spouse, an embrace from a son or daughter, or the firm grasp of a friend, human contact cuts through reasoning and argument and immediately asserts presence and love. Those dealing with hopelessness wait for such contact. Touch is the initial promise that a future is possible.

2) *Hope grows gradually.* One does not leave desolation all at once. One visit by the angel is not enough to provide what Elijah needs. The angel must come twice, repeatedly bringing the nourishment that gives the prophet strength (vv. 5 and 7). Those who are despondent and those who minister to them should not expect a quick reversal. Progress is made through repeated contact, words of support, and prayer. Therefore, patience is a requirement for those who long to hope again. The food the angel brings today is often not enough. Therefore, we may need to wait for his return tomorrow.

3) *The future emerges with time.* Those caught in gloom want to imagine a better future. They must not expect the shape of that future to be clear from the start. As Elijah sits under the broom tree, he plans to stay there until his death. Only at the second visit of the angel is he told there will be a journey (v. 7), and only after he sets out does he realize that his journey will lead to Horeb (v. 8). In the midst of depression, one cannot fret that the future is unknown. The contours of healing appear in stages. Once recovery begins, the future will fall into place. Therefore, in the depths of despondency, the wise option is to eat the food God's angel gives and use the strength it provides to take the next step, a step that will in time lead to blessing.

God knows the depths of despair into which we may fall. Elijah's story in 1 Kings 19 assures us that God will provide us a way out. God's angel will come to touch and feed us as many times as we need and to clarify the journey we are called to take.

Guardian Angels in the Book of Daniel

The first six chapters of the book of Daniel consist of stories about Daniel and his companions during the Jewish exile in Babylon (585–539 BCE). The book itself was composed four hundred years later during the bitter persecution of the Jews by the Greek ruler Antiochus IV Epiphanes (167–164 BCE). In fact, the strategy of the book is to use the older stories of Daniel's faithfulness to address Jews under persecution in a much later period. Daniel's readers are called to remain faithful to God and their Jewish traditions even in the midst of a persecuting pagan culture.

The most famous story in the book of Daniel is the ordeal of Daniel in the lion's den. Daniel, a Jew, is a valued minister of King Darius, the Mede. Other ministers of the king plot against Daniel. They convince the king to forbid the offering of petitions to any god or human except him (Dan 6:5-10). Those who do not obey this command are to be thrown into a den of lions. Even though Daniel is aware of the king's decree, he continues his daily prayers to the God of Israel. When the ministers report this, the king is forced to expose Daniel to the lions. Darius does so reluctantly and hopes that Daniel's God will save him. The story continues:

Daniel 6:19-25

¹⁹Then the king returned to his palace for the night; he refused to eat and he dismissed the entertainers. Since sleep was impossible for him, ²⁰the king rose very early the next morning and hastened to the lions' den. ²¹As he drew near, he cried out to Daniel sorrowfully, "Daniel, servant of the living God, has your God whom you serve so constantly been able to save you from the lions?" ²²Daniel answered the king: "O king, live forever! ²³My God sent his angel and closed the lions' mouths so that they have not hurt me. For I have been found innocent before him; neither have I done you any harm, O king!" ²⁴This gave the king great joy. At his order Daniel was brought up from the den; he was found to be unharmed because he trusted in his God. ²⁵The king then ordered the men who had accused Daniel, along with their children and their wives, to be cast into the lions' den. Before they reached the bottom of the den, the lions overpowered them and crushed all their bones.

Daniel's faith in God is vindicated. God sends a protecting angel to close the mouths of the lions (v. 23). Those who attempted to harm Daniel have no such angel to protect them. Lowered into the den at the king's command, the lions crush "all their bones" (v. 25).

Another story of God's protection occurs in Daniel 3. The pagan king here is Nebuchadnezzar of Babylon. He sets up a golden idol for all in his kingdom to worship (Dan 3:1-7). Three Jews—Shadrach, Meshach, and Abednego—refuse to worship the idol. In a rage, the king orders them thrown into a fiery furnace. But when Nebuchadnezzar looks into the furnace, he is startled and asks his counselors:

Daniel 3:91-92

⁹¹"Did we not cast three men bound into the fire?" "Certainly, O king," they answered. ⁹²"But," he replied, "I see four men unbound and unhurt, walking in the fire, and the fourth looks like a son of God."

God sends an angel (here called "a son of God") to protect the three faithful Jews from the fire. The protection is complete. When the men are pulled out of the furnace, we are told that "not a hair of their heads had been singed, nor were their garments altered; there was not even a smell of fire about them" (Dan 3:94). God's protecting angel not only saves the faithful Jews from death, he even spares them from untidiness!

Contemporary Relevance: We may at first perceive these stories in the book of Daniel as naïve. God protects Daniel and his companions from all harm—even from looking disheveled. But history quickly demonstrates that God's protection is not so simplistic. Acts of genocide are widely documented and have occurred despite fervent prayers for God's protection. Hundreds of thousands of Armenians were killed between 1915 and 1917. Millions of Jews were slaughtered programmatically in the Holocaust. The stories in Daniel were themselves written as thousands of devout Jews were being massacred by Antiochus IV Epiphanes.

A deeper look at Daniel 1–6, however, reveals that the scriptural message is not as naïve as we may first imagine. These stories do not promise that God will magically save all devout believers from death. Shadrach, Meshach, and Abednego say as much to Nebuchadnezzar before he throws them into the furnace in Daniel 3:17-18: "If our God, whom we serve, can save us from the white-hot furnace and from your hands, O king, may he save us! But even if he will not, you should know, O king, that we will not serve your god or worship the golden statue which you set up."

The key to the stories in Daniel, then, is integrity in times of difficulty. Believers are to follow God's commands because they belong to God, no matter what the circumstances. God has the power to send a protecting angel, but being saved from harm is not a condition for faithfulness.

When we face trial and danger, we should not assume that the amazing experience of Daniel, Shadrach, Meshach, and Abednego is guaranteed to us. God has the power to protect us, but we cannot presume that God will always send an angel to keep us from every dis-

tress. God's will and freedom are beyond our understanding. These stories do not promise that we will escape suffering and pain. Instead they provide examples of standing firm in what we know is good and true, in spite of our afflictions. Like believers who faced persecution before us, we are called to profess that God is real and then entrust our lives to God's care.

The realization that God may not always choose to save us from harm is also at the heart of **the story of seven brothers who suffer martyrdom** found in 2 Maccabees 7. All the brothers in this narrative choose to suffer horrific tortures and ultimately death rather than transgress the Mosaic law that forbade them from eating pork. Their perseverance is based on breathtaking fidelity to God and an unwavering trust in God's promise of eternal life for those who are faithful. Like Shadrach, Meshach, and Abednego (Dan 3), the brothers in 2 Maccabees remind us of the need for courageous resolve and immense trust when we face the inevitable tribulations of this life.

The Angel Raphael in the Book of Tobit

The book of Tobit was written in the same time period as the book of Daniel. Like Daniel, its story is set in a much earlier period of Jewish history, in this case Assyria in the seventh century BCE. Tobit is a religious novel offering a narrative for instruction and edification. The story begins with two characters in trouble. Tobit, a devout Jew, has slept in his garden where bird droppings fell into his eyes and rendered him blind (Tob 2:9-10). Sarah, another faithful Jew, has an even greater problem. Over time she has been betrothed to seven husbands, but on each wedding night an evil demon, Asmodeus, has killed each of them. With this history, of course, Sarah can find no one willing to marry her.

Unaware of one another's difficulties, both Tobit and Sarah pray to God from different cities. Their prayers are heard, and God sends the angel Raphael to them:

Tobit 3:16-17

[16]At that very time, the prayer of both of them was heard in the glorious presence of God. [17]So Raphael was sent to heal them both: to remove the white scales from Tobit's eyes, so that he might again see with his own eyes God's light; and to give Sarah, the daughter of Raguel, as a wife to Tobiah, the son of Tobit, and to rid her of the wicked demon Asmodeus.

For the prayers of Tobit and Sarah to be answered, Tobit's son, Tobiah, must journey to Media. He requires a companion and soon encounters Raphael in disguise:

Tobit 5:4-6

[4]Tobiah went out to look for someone who would travel with him to Media, someone who knew the way. He went out and found the angel Raphael standing before him (though he did not know that this was an angel of God). [5]Tobiah said to him, "Where do you come from, young man?" He replied, "I am an Israelite, one of your kindred. I have come here to work." Tobiah said to him, "Do you know the way to Media?" [6]"Yes," he replied, "I have been there many times."

Raphael agrees to travel with Tobiah. The purpose of his presence is not only for guidance to Media but also for protection. Traveling in the ancient world was perilous; only foolish people traveled alone. Tobit assures his wife that their son will return home safely, explaining Raphael's role as guardian:

Tobit 5:21-22

[21] Tobit reassured her: "Do not worry! Our son will leave in good health and come back to us in good health. Your own eyes will see the day when he returns to you safe and sound. So, do not worry; do not fear for them, my sister. [22]For a good angel will go with him, his journey will be successful, and he will return in good health."

Tobit believes that God will provide a guardian angel for his son Tobiah. Part of the irony of the story is that he does not realize that the young man who has just agreed to travel with Tobiah is the angel Raphael.

As the story continues, Raphael directs Tobiah to catch a fish in the Tigris river and save its gall, heart, and liver (6:2-6). In time, Tobiah and Sarah are married, and Tobiah uses the fish's liver and heart to drive away the demon poised to kill him (8:1-3). When Tobiah finally returns to his father's house, he uses a medicine made from the fish's gall to restore Tobit's sight (11:1-15). Shortly thereafter Raphael reveals his identity:

Tobit 12:12, 14-15

[12]"Now when you, Tobit, and Sarah prayed, it was I who presented the record of your prayer before the Glory of the Lord. . . . [14]I was sent to put you to the test. At the same time, however, God sent me to heal you and your daughter-in-law Sarah. [15]I am Raphael, one of the seven angels who stand and serve before the Glory of the Lord."

Contemporary Relevance: The book of Tobit not only describes the ministry of Tobiah's guardian angel, it also tells us the angel's name. Naming angels occurs late in the angelic tradition. In fact, there are only three angels whose names are recorded in the Scriptures: Raphael,

Michael, and Gabriel. *Raphael* is only mentioned in the book of Tobit, where, as we have seen, he plays a major role. *Michael* is presented as the angel protector of Israel in Daniel 10:13, 21; 12:1; argues with the devil in Jude 9; and leads the faithful angels to victory over Satan in Revelation 12:7-9. *Gabriel* is mentioned four times in the Bible. In the book of Daniel, he is sent to help the prophet interpret his visions (8:16 and 9:21); and in the Gospel of Luke, Gabriel announces the birth of John the Baptist and Jesus (1:19 and 1:26).

The Catholic Church celebrates the feast of the archangels—Michael, Gabriel, and Raphael—on September 29. The word "archangel" simply means "leading angel." Only Michael is given this title in the letter of Jude. The tradition, however, has extended the honor to Gabriel and Raphael, because of their prominence in the Scriptures and especially because they are the only other angels who are given names.

When we meet a new person, one of the first things we ask is, "What is your name?" Names distinguish an individual from a general class or grouping. The ability to call a person by his or her own name is a sign of familiarity and respect. The same is true of angels. Even though there are myriads of angelic beings who both guide and protect us, names bring us closer to Raphael, Michael, and Gabriel. In times of need or when we wish to give praise to God, we can use their names to call them to our side.

Raphael identifies himself as "one of the seven angels who stand and serve before the Glory of the Lord" (Tob 12:15). Some scholars interpret the reference to "seven" as a symbolic number that represents totality or completeness, thus understanding Raphael as one among *all* the angels who are granted the privilege of standing before God. Other commentators, however, interpret Raphael's self-description as placing him in the highest class of angels known as **"angels of the presence."** Various lists of these angels and their functions appear in apocryphal texts. One such list appears in 1 Enoch, where the angels are identified as Uriel, Raphael, Raguel, Michael, Saraqael, Gabriel, and Remiel (1 Enoch 20).

Guardian Angels in the New Testament

The ministry of angels as guardians is presented throughout the New Testament, beginning with "guarding" Jesus himself. After his baptism, Jesus confronts Satan in the wilderness. This temptation is recounted in Matthew 4:1-11, Mark 1:12-13, and Luke 4:1-13. Mark's version is brief, whereas Matthew and Luke provide substantial dialogue between Jesus and Satan. In Matthew 4:5-6 (see also Luke 4:9-11), the devil actually tempts Jesus to call upon angels for help:

> ### Matthew 4:5-6
>
> ⁵Then the devil took him to the holy city, and made him stand on the parapet of the temple, ⁶and said to him, "If you are the Son of God, throw yourself down. For it is written:
> 'He will command his angels concerning you'
> and 'with their hands they will support you,
> lest you dash your foot against a stone.'"

The devil is citing Psalm 91, proving, as Shakespeare has written, "The devil can cite scripture for his purpose" (*The Merchant of Venice*, 1.3, 425). Jesus, of course, refuses to accede to Satan's command because he knows it would be a misuse of God's power.

At the end of Jesus' temptations, however, an example of the true ministry of angels is provided. Mark 1:13 says that Jesus "was among wild beasts, and the angels ministered to him." Matthew 4:11 tells us, "Then the devil left him and, behold, angels came and ministered to him." These angels guard and comfort Jesus in the wilderness. Jesus also receives angelic ministry during his passion. Luke's Gospel tells us that "an angel from heaven" appeared to Jesus "to strengthen him" as he prayed on the Mount of Olives (22:43).

The presence of these protecting angels does not save Jesus from temptation, suffering, or death. Such a rescue would of course have been possible. In Matthew 26:53 Jesus tells the disciples in Gethsemane: "Do you think that I cannot call upon my Father and he will not provide me at this moment with more than twelve legions of angels?" Angels could have safeguarded Jesus, but his priority was not his own protection. His mission was to do his Father's will.

In the book of Acts, we read that Paul is also guarded by an angel. Caught in a disastrous storm as he sailed to Rome, Paul assures those on board that they will not die:

Acts 27:22-25

22"I urge you now to keep up your courage; not one of you will be lost, only the ship. 23For last night an angel of the God to whom [I] belong and whom I serve stood by me 24and said, 'Do not be afraid, Paul. You are destined to stand before Caesar; and behold, for your sake, God has granted safety to all who are sailing with you.' 25Therefore, keep up your courage, men; I trust in God that it will turn out as I have been told."

The apostles are also protected by an angel. When the Sanhedrin throws them into jail, God sends an angel to free them:

Acts 5:17-20

17Then the high priest rose up and all his companions, that is, the party of the Sadducees, and, filled with jealousy, 18laid hands upon the apostles and put them in the public jail. 19But during the night, the angel of the Lord opened the doors of the prison, led them out, and said, 20"Go and take your place in the temple area, and tell the people everything about this life."

Even though their ministry places them in danger, the apostles continue to spread the gospel. God's guardian angel protects them and their mission.

Peter's Guardian Angel

Perhaps the most vivid story in the book of Acts is Peter's escape from prison. In this narrative God uses an angel to protect the apostle:

Acts 12:5-17

5Peter thus was being kept in prison, but prayer by the church was fervently being made to God on his behalf.

6On the very night before Herod was to bring him to trial, Peter, secured by double chains, was sleeping between two soldiers, while outside the door guards kept watch on the prison. 7Suddenly the angel of the Lord stood by him and a light shone in the cell. He tapped Peter on the side and awakened him, saying, "Get up quickly." The chains fell from his wrists. 8The angel said to him, "Put on your belt and your sandals." He did so. Then he said to him, "Put on your cloak and follow me." 9So he followed him out, not realizing that what was happening through the angel was real; he thought he was seeing a vision. 10They passed the first guard, then the second, and came to the iron gate leading out to the city, which opened for them by itself. They emerged and made their way down an alley, and suddenly the angel left him. 11Then Peter recovered his senses and said, "Now I know for certain that [the] Lord sent his angel and rescued me from the hand of Herod and from all that the Jewish people had been expecting." 12When he realized this, he went to the house of Mary, the mother of John who is called Mark, where there were many people gathered in prayer. ¹³When he knocked on the gateway door, a maid named Rhoda came to answer it. ¹⁴She was so overjoyed when she recognized Peter's voice that, instead of opening the gate, she ran in and announced that Peter was standing at the gate. ¹⁵They told her, "You are out of your mind," but she insisted that it was so. But they kept saying, "It is his angel." ¹⁶But Peter continued to knock, and when they opened it, they saw him and were astounded. ¹⁷He motioned to them with his hand to be quiet and explained [to them] how the Lord had led him out of the prison, and said, "Report this to James and the brothers." Then he left and went to another place.

Contemporary Relevance: Told with irony and humor, this story engages us. It is also rich with meaning for our lives. Here are two ways this story speaks to our journey of faith.

1) *God protects us when we are unable to protect ourselves.* The first half of this narrative has a dreamlike quality. Peter is in prison, and an angel appears. Peter's chains fall. He and the angel seem to float past the first and second guard and through an iron gate which opens for them on its own accord (vv. 7-10). Peter seems to be in a fog. He follows the angel as if in a dream (v. 9). Only at verse 11 does he recover his senses and realize that he has been rescued by the angel. Like a young child awakened by his parents for a sudden journey, Peter does what he is told without fully understanding what he is doing. In this semi-sleep, the angel is in charge. Notice how gently and carefully he prepares Peter for his release. First he taps Peter and removes his chains (v. 7). Then he tells Peter to dress, first to put on his belt and sandals, then his cloak (v. 8). By the time the angel leaves Peter in an alley and he comes to his senses, Peter is free.

There are times in our lives when we are "in a fog." At times of deep grief, sudden change, or intense sickness, we may find ourselves going through the motions of life without much sense or purpose. We sleepwalk though events, noticing they are happening but somehow not engaged. In those moments we require a special kind of protection. The escape of Peter assures us that although we may be in a haze, we are not without support. God sends an angel to guard and guide us through our choices. The angel tells us, "Put this on. Move this way. Follow as I lead." Although things may be murky for us, God's love and purpose are clear. Step by step God leads us until the fog lifts and we realize we are free.

2) *People may not accept our good news.* Once Peter realizes what God has done in setting him free, a comic irony takes over the story. He goes to where the church is gathered, but he cannot get in. Even though the iron gate of the prison effortlessly opened for him, the gate of Christian assembly remains closed (v. 14). A maid named Rhoda hears Peter's knock and comes to the door. But when she sees Peter,

Deliverance of Saint Peter by an angel. Wood engraving after a fresco by Raphael (1483–1520) in the Stanza della Segnatura, Apostolic Palace, Vatican, published in 1884.

Rhoda is so overcome with joy that she runs in to tell everyone that Peter is free and forgets to unlock the door! The assembly refuses to accept Rhoda's announcement, saying, "You are out of your mind" (v. 15).

These verses drip with irony. The community tells Rhoda that she has only seen Peter's "angel," supposing she was having a vision (v. 15), but Peter is waiting at the gate because his real guardian angel has freed him! The gathered church continues to pray for Peter (vv. 5 and 12), but the answer to their prayers is already standing at their door. Despite the best efforts of Peter and Rhoda, the community will not listen. They refuse to let the good news in.

When God has blessed us, led us to a new insight, or set us on a new path, we want to tell our good news to others. We should not be surprised if our announcement is not always immediately received. Even though we can say with confidence, "I love you. I forgive you. I need you. I can help you," we may find ourselves with Peter, standing in an alley before a locked gate. Good news is not always embraced.

Interestingly, Luke seems to have modeled the announcement of Peter's escape on the announcement of Jesus' resurrection. When Mary Magdalene, Joanna, and Mary the mother of James bring the joyful news of the empty tomb to the gathered disciples, we are told that "their story seemed like nonsense and they did not believe them" (Luke 24:11). The initial response to the world's greatest news was also rejected.

Yet the story of Peter's escape offers hope. Even as the community refuses to believe, Peter continues to knock (v. 16). In time the door is opened, and the community believes. We should not become discouraged by initial rejection or disbelief. In time, people may come to see that our love, forgiveness, and offer to help is real. Eventually people accepted the words and witness of the women at the tomb, Rhoda, and Peter. Our announcements can also be received. Continue to knock.

The Guardian Angel of the Holy Family

The most elaborate scriptural narrative about a guardian angel is found in the infancy narrative of Matthew. Over two chapters, through five scenes, an angel appears three times to Joseph in order to protect the Holy Family. The first intervention takes place before Jesus' birth:

Matthew 1:18-25.

[18]Now this is how the birth of Jesus Christ came about. When his mother Mary was betrothed to Joseph, but before they lived together, she was found with child through the holy Spirit. [19]Joseph her husband, since he was a righteous man, yet unwilling to expose her to shame, decided to divorce her quietly. [20]Such was his intention when, behold, the angel of the Lord appeared to him in a dream and said, "Joseph, son of David, do not be afraid to take Mary your wife into your home. For it is through the holy Spirit that this child has been conceived in her. [21]She will bear a son and you are to name him Jesus, because he will save his people from their sins." [22]All this took place to fulfill what the Lord had said through the prophet:

[23]"Behold, the virgin shall be with child and
   bear a son,
 and they shall name him Emmanuel,"
which means "God is with us." [24]When Joseph awoke, he did as the angel of the Lord had commanded him and took his wife into his home. [25]He had no relations with her until she bore a son, and he named him Jesus.

When Joseph cannot understand Mary's pregnancy and prepares to divorce her, an angel assures him that God is at work. The message guards the Holy Family, for without the marriage of Joseph and Mary, there would be no family in which Jesus could live and grow.

After Jesus' birth, magi come to visit the Christ Child (2:1-12). They inform Herod of the birth of Jesus, which initiates his plan to kill the child. As the magi leave, an angel appears to Joseph for the second time:

Matthew 2:13-15

¹³When they had departed, behold, the angel of the Lord appeared to Joseph in a dream and said, "Rise, take the child and his mother, flee to Egypt, and stay there until I tell you. Herod is going to search for the child to destroy him." ¹⁴Joseph rose and took the child and his mother by night and departed for Egypt. ¹⁵He stayed there until the death of Herod, that what the Lord had said through the prophet might be fulfilled, "Out of Egypt I called my son."

Jesus is safe in Egypt when Herod slaughters the male children in Bethlehem and its surroundings (2:16-18). Time passes, and Herod dies. Then an angel appears to Joseph a third time:

Matthew 2:19-23

¹⁹When Herod had died, behold, the angel of the Lord appeared in a dream to Joseph in Egypt ²⁰and said, "Rise, take the child and his mother and go to the land of Israel, for those who sought the child's life are dead." ²¹He rose, took the child and his mother, and went to the land of Israel. ²²But when he heard that Archelaus was ruling over Judea in place of his father Herod, he was afraid to go back there. And because he had been warned in a dream, he departed for the region of Galilee. ²³He went and dwelt in a town called Nazareth, so that what had been spoken through the prophets might be fulfilled, "He shall be called a Nazorean."

Contemporary Relevance: This lengthy story assures us that God's protection is not limited by circumstance, time, or place. The angel protects the Holy Family through a variety of circumstances: the confusion of Joseph (1:20), a threat from Herod (2:13), and the journey to a new home (2:20). The work of the angel is not restricted to a specific time. It addresses circumstances before Jesus birth, during Herod's threat, and after Herod's death. The angel affects events in numerous places: Bethlehem, Egypt, Judea, and Nazareth.

The angel of the Holy Family reminds us that there is no time or place that can separate us from God's care and protecting angels. This story reflects the comforting message of Psalm 139:7-10:

> ⁷Where can I go from your spirit?
>   From your presence, where can I flee?
> ⁸If I ascend to the heavens, you are there;
>   if I lie down in Sheol, there you are.
> ⁹If I take the wings of dawn
>   and dwell beyond the sea,
> ¹⁰Even there your hand guides me,
>   your right hand holds me fast.

We cannot elude God's presence and protection. Even if we take the wings of the dawn, God is there. Even if we dwell beyond the sea, God's angels still guard us.

Our Guardian Angels

Most of the passages we have examined in this lesson present guardian angels in specific circumstances: the depression of Elijah, the threats to Daniel and his companions, the journey of Tobiah, the temptation and passion of Jesus, the escape of Peter. A few of the stories we have discussed, however, hint at something more. Jacob, looking over his life, mentions an angel who has protected him from all harm—not just in one circumstance but in many. The Holy Family also depends on an angel guardian who accompanies them through many events. Such stories reflect a belief that was gaining acceptance at the time of Jesus: the existence of a guardian angel who abides with each person. Many Jewish works speak of angels who are not only sent when they are needed but who remain with individuals always. Such a belief may well have developed from the idea of angelic powers (see Lesson Four). Just as nations and elements of the natural world were seen to have an angel to rule them, so individuals could be seen to have an angel to guard them.

There is only one passage in the New Testament that mentions personal guardian angels. Before Jesus tells the parable of the lost sheep in the Gospel of Matthew, he says to his disciples: "See that you do not despise one of these little ones, for I say to you that their angels in heaven always look upon the face of my heavenly Father" (18:10). Anxious to admonish his disciples to care for the most vulnerable members of the community (the "little ones"), Jesus uses angels to stress the value of the least among us. He says that the little ones—like all of us—have spiritual guardians who see God's face.

The belief in personal guardian angels was quickly accepted by the church fathers and became a part of Catholic belief. Citing St. Basil, the *Catechism of the Catholic Church* states: "Beside each believer stands an angel as protector and shepherd leading him to life" (336).

Contemporary Relevance: The belief that God has assigned each of us our own guardian angel is a deep source of comfort. With all the needs and crises in the world, we may fear that the issues of our lives will be lost amongst all the hardships that God is asked to address. Such a fear is, of course, unfounded. God is fully capable of responding to the prayers of every person. Yet the image of a guardian angel standing at our side allows us to visualize the presence of God who is always with us. As we envision our guardian angel accompanying us as Raphael accompanied Tobias, strengthening us as the angel strengthened Elijah, and blessing us throughout our lives as Jacob's angel blessed him, we remember that we are never alone. God has loved us enough to personalize that love in our own angelic companion.

* * * * * *

The belief in a personal guardian angel is an appropriate place to end our study. We have traced the development of angels from early scriptural passages in which the presence of an angel "slipped" into the presence of God. We have explored descriptions of angels that ranged from the mundane to the exotic. We have discussed the ministries of angels as those who adore God, speak for God, rule the cosmos, and judge the world. But the most comforting ministry of angels is their ministry of walking with us as the guardians of our lives. Such protection gives us confidence and hope. And by now we fully understand that this constant protection we experience from angels is in fact the shelter of our loving God.

An angel strengthens Elijah.

EXPLORING LESSON SIX

1. What reasons might there have been for Jacob to cross his hands in blessing his grandsons Ephraim and Manasseh (Gen 48:8-20)? Which reason do you find most convincing?

_____

_____

_____

_____

_____

_____

2. Did you find the story of Elijah and the angel helpful in facing times of depression, either for yourself or a loved one (1 Kgs 19:1-8)? If so, in what way? If not, why?

_____

_____

_____

_____

_____

_____

3. In discussing the stories of protection in Daniel 1–6, the lesson states that "being saved from harm is not a condition for faithfulness." How do you understand this?

_____

_____

_____

_____

_____

4. Who are the only three angels named in the Bible, and what is the significance of their names being known?

_____

_____

_____

_____

_____

5. Raphael's role in the book of Tobit has made him not only a patron of travelers but a patron of those in need of healing. Have you or someone you know experienced God's healing in a time of sickness? Are you willing to share the story?

_____

_____

_____

_____

_____

_____

6. In what two events of Jesus' life does he receive the ministry of angels, and what was the purpose of these angelic visitations (Mark 1:13; Matt 4:11; Luke 22:43)?

_____

_____

_____

_____

_____

7. The commentary on Peter's escape from prison (Acts 12:5-17) highlighted several ways of interpreting the text for our own spiritual lives. Did either of these approaches resonate with you? What insights did you gain from reading and reflecting on this passage?

_____

_____

_____

_____

_____

_____

8. In what three circumstances was an angel sent to Joseph to aid the Holy Family (Matt 1:18-25; 2:13-15, 19-23)?

_____

_____

_____

_____

_____

9. How do you understand the role of a guardian angel? Has this study changed your understanding of who your guardian angel is?

_____

_____

_____

_____

_____

10. Reflect on all you have learned and reflected on during your study of angels in the Bible. What emerges as the most valuable thing you learned or the most meaningful thing you have applied to your life with God?

_____

_____

_____

_____

_____

CLOSING PRAYER

Prayer

"Blessed be God,
 blessed be his great name,
  and blessed be all his holy angels.
May his great name be with us,
  and blessed be all the angels throughout all
   the ages."   (Tob 11:14)

May our praise of God be unceasing, and may our thanks for God's many favors be joyful and sincere. Like the heavenly hosts of angels, may we express the depth of our devotion by being God's faithful ministers on earth. Today let us especially express our zeal for God's name by . . .

PRAYING WITH YOUR GROUP

Because we know that the Bible allows us to hear God's voice, prayer provides the context for our study and sharing. By speaking and listening to God and each other, the discussion often grows to more deeply bond us to one another and to God.

At *the beginning and end of each lesson* simple prayers are provided for individual use, and also may be used within the group setting. Most of the closing prayers provided with each lesson relate directly to a theme from that lesson and encourage you to pray together for people and events in your local community.

Of course, there are many ways to center ourselves in God's presence as we gather together in groups around the word of God. We provide some additional suggestions here knowing you and your group will make prayer a priority as part of your gathering. These are simply alternative ways to pray if your group would like to try something different from those prayers provided in the previous pages.

Conversational Prayer

This form of prayer allows for the group members to pray in their own words in a way that is not intimidating. The group leader begins with Step One, inviting all to focus on the presence of Christ among them. After a few moments of quiet, the group leader invites anyone in the group to voice a prayer or two of thanksgiving; once that is complete, then anyone who has personal intentions may pray in their own words for their needs; finally, the group prays for the needs of others.

A suggested process:
In your own words, speak simple and short prayers to allow time for others to add their voices.

Focus on one "step" at a time, not worrying about praying for everything in your mental list at once.

Step One	Visualize Christ. Welcome him. Imagine him present with you in your group. Allow time for some silence.
Step Two	Gratitude opens our hearts. Use simple words such as, "Thank you, Lord, for . . ."
Step Three	Pray for your own needs knowing that others will pray with you. Be specific and honest. Use "I" and "me" language.

Step Four   Pray for others by name, with love.
                          You may voice your agreement ("Yes, Lord").
                          End with gratitude for sharing concerns.

Praying Like Ignatius

St. Ignatius Loyola, whose life and ministry are the foundation of the Jesuit community, invites us to enter into Scripture texts in order to experience the scenes, especially scenes of the gospels or other narrative parts of Scripture. Simply put, this is a method of creatively imagining the scene, viewing it from the inside, and asking God to meet you there. Most often, this is a personal form of prayer, but in a group setting, some of its elements can be helpful if you allow time for this process.

A suggested process:

- Select a scene from the chapters in the particular lesson.
- Read that scene out loud in the group, followed by some quiet time.
- Ask group members to place themselves in the scene (as a character, or as an onlooker) so that they can imagine the emotions, responses, and thinking that may have taken place. Notice the details and the tone, and imagine the interaction with the Lord that is taking place.
- Share with the group any insights that came to you in this quiet imagining.
- Allow each person in the group to thank God for some insight and to pray about some request that may have surfaced.

Sacred Reading (or Lectio Divina)

This method of prayer invites us to "listen with the ear of the heart" as St. Benedict's rule would say. We listen to the words and the phrasing, asking God to speak to our innermost being. Again, this method of prayer is most often used in an individual setting but may also be used in an adapted way within a group.

A suggested process:

- Select a scene from the chapters in the particular lesson.
- Read the scene out loud in the group, perhaps two times.
- Ask group members to ponder a word or phrase that stands out to them.
- The group members could then simply speak the word or phrase as a kind of litany of what was meaningful for your group.
- Allow time for more silence to ponder the words that were heard, asking God to reveal to you what message you are meant to hear, how God is speaking to you.
- Follow up with spoken intentions at the close of this group time.

REFLECTING ON SCRIPTURE

Reading Scripture is an opportunity not simply to learn new information but to listen to God who loves you. Pray that the same Holy Spirit who guided the formation of Scripture will inspire you to correctly understand what you read, and empower you to make what you read a part of your life.

The inspired word of God contains layers of meaning. As you make your way through passages of Scripture, whether studying a book of the Bible or focusing on a biblical theme, you may find it helpful to ask yourself these four questions:

What does the Scripture passage say?
Read the passage slowly and reflectively. Become familiar with it. If the passage you are reading is a narrative, carefully observe the characters and the plot. Use your imagination to picture the scene or enter into it.

What does the Scripture passage mean?
Read the footnotes in your Bible and the commentary provided to help you understand what the sacred writers intended and what God wants to communicate by means of their words.

What does the Scripture passage mean to me?
Meditate on the passage. God's word is living and powerful. What is God saying to you? How does the Scripture passage apply to your life today?

What am I going to do about it?
Try to discover how God may be challenging you in this passage. An encounter with God contains a challenge to know God's will and follow it more closely in daily life. Ask the Holy Spirit to inspire not only your mind but your life with this living word.